Contents

WITH SPECIAL GUEST APPEARANCES FROM:

Tiki Barber
Joe Bell
Joe Benigno
Mike Breen
Chris Carlin
Craig Carton
Mark Chernoff
Gary Dell'Abate
Bo Dietl
Scott Ferrall
Mike Francesa
Artie Lange
Mark Lepselter
Mike Levy
Jackie "the Jokeman" Martling
Bernard McGuirk
Phil Mushnick
Jim Nantz
Pat Riley
Chris Russo
Steve Schirripa
Lesley Visser

Foreword

From 1995 to 1997 I was on Fox's *MADtv*, a sketch comedy show. That was sort of my break into show business. The show was successful in the sense that it stayed on the air for 14 years—I think it's the second-longest-running sketch show ever. During the first couple of years we were happy to be on television and making decent money, but no one was looking for us to be a guest on any certain talk show, unless we did standup or something. I was doing a gig down in the Florida area when my agent called me up and said, "You know, there's a sports show out of Miami called *Scott and Sid*. They want to have you on and do an interview." I had never really been on the radio before. I was 27 years old and had been on *MADtv* for a few months, and I quickly agreed. "Great, I'll plug the standup gig, *MADtv*, whatever."

I called into the show, and they were both great guys. They were both funny, and we had a great conversation about sports. They got all my crazy sports references that I couldn't make anywhere else, and we laughed for something like like a half an hour. I ended up calling in a couple more times. Once they came up to New York to do a remote broadcast from CBS in the control room during the first weekend of the NCAA Tournament, and I went on their show live, met them face to face, and we just laughed and had a blast.

I always thought Sid was hilarious. I lost contact with him over time, and then I was on *The Howard Stern Show* and I heard Sid Rosenberg was on *Imus*. I said, "That's the Sid that I did that show with." Of course Stern and the *Imus* show were at odds with one another—and I'm in Howard's army forever. But even Howard's producer Gary Dell'Abate says Sid's a good guy, because they knew each other. I told him, "I love Sid. He's funny as hell." He sort of did what I did but on *Imus*. He had his issues with drugs just like me. We just had a lot in common. So I contacted Sid again, we started talking, and we became good friends. He wanted to come on with Stern after he got fired from *Imus*, and Howard was a little reluctant. Gary and I both worked on Howard. I told him, "Howard, this guy is a funny guy, a huge fan of yours, I've known him for a long time, and he's got amazing stories about Imus and drugs." Howard loves honesty. Gary and I were both instrumental in getting Sid on, and when he came on he was fantastic. Howard loved him. He even used him for a few things on Howard TV.

Sid obviously is a loyal guy. I know what that's like. I wouldn't fuck with Howard for anything or anyone in the world. Sid might well have that feeling toward Imus. He's led an interesting life, he came on and was honest about other things, and he was great. He's funny, I think he's very talented, I think he's great on the radio. Whenever I had a gig in Miami or a book signing, I called in to his show there and we'd have a blast. Sid's the best.

You know, there are people who have led way less interesting lives who have written a book. I'd rather read Sid's book than Paris Hilton's Twitter. I wrote *Too Fat to Fish*, and I didn't think I'd ever *read* a book. Actually, I enjoy reading a lot, and I always wanted to write a book. After a few years on the Stern show, book agents started to call me every day. I guess I have a lot of crazy, fucked-up stories—that's how I got on *Howard*. When I got that job, I made a conscious decision just to be honest, like Richard Pryor, to try to be funny that way. And it got me a book deal. For me, talking about all my fuckups with drugs and everything else, was very, very cathartic and therapeutic. It worked for me, so I said to Sid, "As a friend of yours, I'm glad you're doing this because it's helpful."

Listen, this politically correct bullshit that's still going on all over the world right now—99 percent of the people in the world don't think that way. There's a small enclave in Malibu and the Hamptons that think that way. Everyone else likes people to joke around the way that they always have. It doesn't mean you hate anybody; it means you're having fun. Sid has that edgy kind of humor—and believe me, there's a market for it. I'm living proof of that. I don't apologize for anything I say if it's a joke. I'm not a racist. I have no hatred for anyone in the world in my heart. I'm a comedian. Look, if a joke's bad I'll apologize for it, but I won't apologize if I offend somebody. Sid's a talented guy and the same way. Look at Howard: he is insanely talented, but of course he's smart. Howard has said things that are politically incorrect, and gotten attention for it.

I remember we had some joke in the movie I was in, *Beer League*, that somebody thought was racist. One of the producers was worried that we might get protestors. I said, "If we get protestors I'm going to fucking high-five every one of them." That's the greatest publicity you can get. As a performer like Sid—or me or Howard or anybody like us—the worst sin you can commit is to be boring. And Sid ain't boring.

—Artie Lange
Comedian, *The Howard Stern Show*

Introduction

I'm not great at a lot of things.

I have not been the perfect husband. I love my wife as much as any other husband out there, but I have put my family in some very tough spots. I think I'm a really good father. But I'm not great at anything, including sex. The one time I'm close to great is when that "On Air" light is on for four hours a day. I'm close to great—no, I think I am great, actually. I mean, I'm not Howard Stern, I'm not Don Imus, and I'm not Rush Limbaugh, but in my field I think I'm great. Because of that, I have an unquenchable thirst to do more and more. In this arena I have a huge sense of self.

But I'm incredibly insecure about everything else. I'm scared to do anything else in life. I need help. I'm nervous. I'm anxious. But when that red light goes on, for those four hours I'm the fucking king of the jungle, man. I don't give a fuck who you are, I'm going to make you entertaining, I'm going to make you interesting, and you're not going to intimidate me.

What separates me from everybody else in this business? You think Mike Francesa is great, you think Joe Rose is great, you think Craig Carton is great, you think Jim Rome is great, you think Dan Patrick is great? First of all, a lot of these guys haven't had the problems I've had. Sure, some of them have, and some of them have had other problems, but what separates me from the pack is I actually talk about it. I don't treat this job like, "Hey, it's four hours. You have shit going on in your life and so do I, so let's escape and talk about the New York Giants." When I got back from rehab and Imus put me back in the studio after 30 days, I sat with the rabbi and the priest and I cried. Not long before that, I was about to jump off a hotel room balcony in Cleveland. I'm not saying that my checkered past is appealing to listeners or that it's the reason they like me—because I think you have to be talented and good at what you do first—but if you can keep their interest and at the same time admit some of your vulnerabilities and flaws and have people identify with you, then it does enhance your persona.

If you asked people, "Do you know Mike Francesa?" they would say, "I know he likes the Yankees. I know he knows about sports." Ask them, "Do you know Chris Russo?" and they'd say, "Yeah, he likes to play tennis." They don't *know* them. I think people know me. And listen, some of them hate me for it. They think I'm the scum of the earth, the fact that I talk about this stuff when I've got a wife, I've got kids. *Where's my shame?* they ask.

Can I be happy? No, I can't. I've gone to enough shrinks and therapists to figure this out. How could I possibly be happy? I have a gorgeous, beautiful, and doting wife. I've got two great children. I've made more than a million dollars. I had the best job in the world at WFAN, and I've had two great jobs since. I have great parents, family, and friends. So how do you explain somebody who's done everything he can to sabotage all of it? Someone who's been in rehab twice? Someone who has a gambling problem? They say in the meetings that when things are going really badly, that seems a good time to go and blow your brains out. The scary part is that when things are going really, really well, it's also a great time to go out and blow your brains out. That's kind of been me. I've been diagnosed bipolar, and I've had my share of ups and downs. I've never been able to find that middle ground. I've never done anything in moderation, including my job. My job is an 18-hour-a-day job. I never did drugs in moderation, I never gambled in moderation, I never drank in moderation. I have never done my show in moderation, either. With me, everything is full-speed ahead. As a result, I'm left with little time to enjoy anything.

No, it's not good. No, it's not okay. In the end, I think that's why I've been so self-destructive. Very rarely am I happy. I'm always looking for, wanting, and expecting more. What happened with my father this past summer, when he got really sick in July, has caused me to feel a little differently now than I have in my whole life. I now try at least a couple of times a day to sit down, take a deep breath, take a look where I am, take a look at my house, my wife, my kids, and think to myself, *Wow, you really have it pretty good. You have a pretty nice life*. I think I'm better now than I've been in my whole life, but it's still not great.

I'm afraid of complacency. I've been told, "Go take medication." I was on antidepressants for a while and I was tired and I was lethargic, common side effects of mood-altering drugs. I told my wife, Danielle, I don't have a regular 9-to-5 job where I can afford to be a little tired in the morning. That fucking light goes on at 6:00 in the morning, and I have to be funny and energetic. I have to be ready to go. I don't think my life powers down—that's my problem.

I've lived a chaotic existence. Part of it is because I'm a crazy person, I'll be the first to admit it. The last thing I want is for people to pick up this book 20 years from now and say, "Wow, things haven't changed." There was a time in my career when the old adage "any publicity is good publicity" rang true to me. Some of the stuff people thought was horrifying and horrible—well, they can say whatever they want, but the fact is I've been fired and they've called me back a week later. I enjoyed my greatest success at WFAN after that type of stuff. There *was* a point in my career where bad publicity was good publicity. When *Time* magazine dubbed me the "Loser of the Month," things got better. I was picked in between Slobodan Milosevic and Osama Bin Laden in that category. But it's over now for me. I can't get the bad publicity anymore. I can't afford it. People have had enough.

My Big Break Into Radio, or How I Won Over the I-Man to Become an *Imus* Regular

When I was a little boy attending Poly Prep in Brooklyn, my father had Don Imus on every morning when he drove me to school. I distinctly remember it—I must have been only 12 years old, listening to *Imus*. I didn't like it—I wanted to listen to music. I was a kid. I remember this bit in which a couple was having sex—it was a "history of the world" theme or something. Imus used to have these bits in which he explained things that happened in history. In this particular bit, he was explaining why the Hindenburg blew up. I was just learning in school at that time about the Hindenburg, so my ears pricked up. In this bit this guy is having sex with this girl in the bow of the Hindenburg, kind of like Leonardo DiCaprio and Kate Winslet in *Titanic*. They finish having sex and the guy says, "Oh man, that was great. God, I could really use a cigarette." She says, "Me too." So they light the cigarette and of course the fucking thing blows up. I remember thinking it was beyond brilliant.

I had met Mark Chernoff, the WFAN program director, at Rockefeller Center. Mike and the Mad Dog were doing a show outside by the ice skating rink during the 2000 Mets-Yankees World Series. I kind of called him over and said, "Hi, Mr. Chernoff. You don't know who I am, but my name is Sid Rosenberg. I do mornings at WNEW." Turns out he did know who I was. And, as I came to discover, he, along with Lee Davis and a couple of other people at the FAN, knew who I was because they were listening. I was doing a sports show, the ratings weren't there, and nobody really knew about us—but they were listening. And they liked my work, I knew that. I was going back and forth with other people at the FAN who told me for a fact Chernoff and Lee Davis thought I was good.

So my agent called them out of the blue and said, "Listen, Sid's leaving WNEW. He's probably going to go back to Florida, but he'd love to work at the FAN. What do you think?" At the time the FAN had no day openings because they had Imus, Jody McDonald and Suzyn Waldman middays, and then Mike and the Mad Dog. Chernoff said to my agent that day that there was a brand-new TV thing called YES for the Yankees and that he had it on good authority that Suzyn Waldman was going to leave and go to work for George Steinbrenner at YES. Chernoff said, "Once she does, middays will go to Sid. I promise when she leaves, Sid will have that job." My agent said, "Wow, that's great, but what are we going to do now? He's leaving a six-figure job at WNEW. He can't just do weekends for $300 a pop." Chernoff said, "At least until I can put him in middays, to get him some money and keep him on the air, how about he goes to *Imus*?" At the time, Imus was using John Minko and Warner Wolf. Chernoff thought my dynamic would be good for Imus because I was kind of young, I was brasher, and I had more attitude. That's what they wanted to bring to sports. Mike Breen was there, and he was really funny. They thought I could be the next best thing.

When my agent called me, I was like, "*Imus*? Jesus Christ. You kidding me? *Imus*?" So Chernoff orchestrated the way in which I would meet Imus. It was May, and they were doing the radiothon show. I had been out of WNEW for about a month, and Chernoff told me, "Show up for the day, come in the morning, and when the *Imus* show is over you'll walk up to Don. I'll introduce the two of you guys, and then you'll say hello and you'll start on his show in a couple of weeks." They started me off doing one day a week on the

Imus show. That was the deal, just Tuesdays. I went down to Rockefeller Center, and Mike Francesa—who I've never met before, though I've been a fan my entire life—walked up to me and gave me a couple of pointers. Mike Breen was there that day. He gave me a couple of pointers, too. Now mind you, I didn't know these guys, had never met them before. I wasn't sure if they even knew me, but they were all very nice.

Sure enough, the show ended, and Imus was up on stage in the basement of Rockefeller Center. He started walking off the stage, put his cowboy hat on, grabbed his briefcase, and Chernoff started nudging me, "C'mon, c'mon, c'mon, c'mon." So I went over to Chernoff and started to follow Imus out of the building. He walked toward the escalator on his way out of the building and Chernoff couldn't get Imus to acknowledge me. Eventually he says, "Imus, this is Sid Rosenberg. He starts with you next week." Imus looked down at me, tipped his cowboy hat, looked up, and walked out. There was nothing there.

I walked out thinking, *Oh my God, he hates me*. It wasn't as if he said, "Hey, it'll be great to have you next week." It wasn't even as if he said, "Get the fuck out of here, kid." It was more like, "Who the fuck are you, and why are you wasting my time?" I remember saying to Chernoff afterward, "Oh man, this is not going to work. Did you see how he acted there?" Cherny replied, "Don't worry. He's like that with everybody the first time they meet him."

Two weeks later at 6:00 in the morning on a Tuesday I was in the studio with the guy. Early on, it was very uncomfortable. You have to understand that it wasn't Imus who picked me. I always thought early on Imus kind of—I don't want to say he resented me, that's a bit strong, but it was sort of like I was forced on Imus by Chernoff. Maybe forced is even too strong a word, but at the end of the day I was only there because Chernoff wanted me to be at the station. He knew early on that he had to get me shifts and get me involved. It definitely wasn't Imus saying, "Hey, I heard that guy Sid. He's really good." He had no idea who the fuck I was. For starters, we were on the same time in the morning. Secondly he would never have listened to my show because it was a sports show. Then all of a sudden I'm popping up on his show. The Imus fraternity—Bernard McGuirk has been there for more than 20 years, Charles McCord has been there for 20-plus years, Rob Bartlett, Larry Kenney, Lou Rufino—has been together forever. To have some fucking loudmouth jerk show up out of nowhere, I'm sure Imus thought, *What the fuck is this?* Chernoff kept telling him "Trust me. He's funny, he's quick-witted, he's opinionated." It was uncomfortable for a couple of months, and then a month into it, in June 2000, I had the Venus and Serena Williams slipup. That brought Imus and me together very quickly, because he fired me—for the first time.

I've been back and forth with the guy four times in nine years. I worked from June 2000 to 2005 full time, starting off doing 10 minutes of sports. Eventually, unlike Mike Breen or Patrick McEnroe or anybody else who did sports (Chris Russo also did sports for Imus, and so did Mike Francesa), my 10-minute sports update evolved, and I ended up in Imus' studio for four hours a day. During my sports report we would delve into myriad topics outside the world of sports. Any sports topic could quickly take us down the path of entertainment. I was even involved in his political interviews. Eventually he wanted me in there just like a cast member, like Bernie or anybody else. I would walk out after sports, and he'd get pissed at me. They'd show my seat on TV and it would be empty, and Imus would yell, "Where the hell is Sid?" He wanted me in there for the whole show. I was the only guy in the history of that role that did that for him.

In fact, even before the Rutgers incident, when I was off FAN, I filled in for Chris Carlin during the week of the Super Bowl. I was already doing the midday show down in Florida. Carlin was on vacation for the Super Bowl down in Miami—it was the Bears and the Colts—and I got a call from Chernoff asking if I'd be willing to fill in for the week to do some sports on *Imus*. I went down to the convention center in Miami where I was doing my show—that's where Radio Row was for the Super Bowl—at something like 5:00 in the morning, did *Imus* from 5:30 to 10:00, and then did my show from 10:00–1:00 PM. It went really well with Imus, and we started talking about me coming back full time and not just in a sports role. Carlin would continue doing sports, and I would be in studio like Bernie as a regular cast member, commenting on anything and everything—which was what my role had evolved into before I left anyway. The idea was great. I flew up a couple of times, to be in the studio. I went to see *The Sopranos* premiere at Radio City, and I was live up in New York for that for Imus. I had started doing his show more and more, and then of course the Rutgers incident happened. I was on the air that day, too, and that was the end of that.

I like Imus. You have to be crazy. Certainly anybody who is as successful as Don has been in the entertainment world is required to be crazy. I don't care what anybody tells you—it requires smarts and other things along the way, but it also requires some crazy. Sure, he can be extremely caustic, and he can be a pain in the ass. There were a lot of mornings when Don would come in and he didn't want to see me and I didn't want to see him. That's just the way it was. But at the end of the day, working for Don was incredibly rewarding. I can't believe I'm living 1,300 miles away from New York and more than four years off that show. I haven't been on MSNBC for four years, and yet I still get stopped almost every single day in Boca, and somebody will say to me, "Hey, you're the guy from *Imus*." I'm just amazed how far-reaching it is. It's a very, very influential show. He's a little quirky and a lot mercurial, but in the end he's very loyal. He's proven that to me, at least.

I'm Not Saying that Cleveland Is a Bad Place, but It Sure Was for Me

It started when I was in high school. I'd go out with a bunch of buddies, head to a nightclub in the city and we'd be able to dance until 5:00 in the morning. That was the extent of it. Look, the first time you do it there's a definite feeling of invincibility, like, *I'm Superman. I can do anything*. If you felt like you didn't look good that night, all of a sudden you're lookin' great. If you'd felt a little tired that night, all of a sudden you were supercharged. Whenever we went into Manhattan, we knew that three things were going to happen: we were going to go to a club, we were going to have a couple of drinks, and we were going to do some blow. That's just the way it was.

I went to high school between 1980 and 1984, pretty much the height of the cocaine craze. The first time I did a lot of cocaine was as a junior in high school, just 16 years old. By the time I was a senior, my friends and I were heading to Manhattan on weekends and partying at different clubs. One place I went to quite a bit was the Underground, on 17th and Broadway. But we went to all the clubs back then: Bedrock's, Flinstone's, Xenon, Merlin's, the Limelight. Probably twice a month, I'd go out on a Friday night and snort cocaine. It was everywhere. It was easy to get. If you ran out, you could usually go downstairs and buy some in the bathroom. That's how it was back then. And I primarily did it to keep myself up. At 5:00 in the morning, when most of the people were headed home, there were only three or four people still dancing on the dance floor—those were the people who were all juiced up.

It wasn't as if I was doing $1,000 of the stuff a day. I put a couple of hundred bucks aside for the weekend, to go to a club in the city on a Friday night. If that didn't last, your buddies bought it for you. Most people who do drugs hang out with people who also do drugs. That way, they avoid the judgment of anyone saying, "Eww, that's gross." When you're getting high, you want people to party along with you. If you have four or five guys going out and they all do it, then for a hundred or two hundred bucks, you're good to go. There were plenty of times in my life where I'd go six, seven, eight months and wouldn't even go near cocaine. But if I started on a Friday, it usually was going to be a marathon weekend.

Throughout my life I've always been a recreational drug user—a binge guy and a weekend warrior. Contrary to what some people think, I never once showed up for work—Imus or FAN or anywhere else—drunk or on drugs. Ever. Part of the reason I got into trouble with Imus was that I would call in at 5:00 or 6:00 AM and say, "Hey, I'm really fucked up. I don't think I can come in today." Usually the recommendation was, "Just get here. Throw on a pair of sunglasses, take a shower, and just get to work." I just couldn't do it. I was so anxious and nervous because I knew I was fucked up. Through high school to working with my father through when I first got married to the last 11 or 12 years on radio, it was never something I did during the week. It was never something I needed to go to work, either. The real problem was that some of those binges that started on a Friday night wouldn't stop until Monday morning. There were a lot of weekends in my life during which I was up for 48 straight hours before it was time to go back to school to work. Those times were tough.

My stay at the University of Miami lasted only three months because all I did every single day was do coke and eat Cap'n Crunch.

I never went to class. I went to Miami premed, got there in August and came home in November. I had lost almost 30 pounds. I was pretty sick. I was effectively quarantined in my basement in Brooklyn when I got back because I literally did not eat for something like a month and a half. My family had come down to see me in Miami in October, and they immediately knew that something was up because I looked awful. By the time I came home in November, I was barely recognizable.

It took me seven years and four different schools to get through college. I started at Miami. Then I went to Brooklyn College—that was a total disaster. After Brooklyn College, I thought my collegiate career was basically over. I had no credits from Miami, and I had nothing to show for Brooklyn College, either. But my mom did some research and found out about a program at Kingsborough Community College that was a second-chance deal. There I started to (at least) go to class and get my grades. I went there and got my associate's degree and did what I had to do. Eventually, I went to Baruch College, where I got my bachelor's degree in business administration.

It got out of hand a couple of times. I had to go to rehab in 1995, after being married for about three years. I went to a rehab place in Pennsylvania, Chit Chat Farms in Wernersville, up by Reading. It's a horrible place. That was one of the worst days of my life. I was leaving that day—my parents actually were going to drive me up to Pennsylvania—and it ended up being the same day my wife graduated from Brooklyn College. So that morning I got all dressed up and went to the college to watch my wife's graduation. Hillary Clinton spoke that day. It was a big day for my wife, a proud day. Then, as soon as the graduation was over, I gave her a kiss goodbye and left.

I had had a couple of really, really rough weeks leading up to this. My wife had had enough. At the time, I was working two jobs. I was working for my father —he's a chemical engineer. He makes water treatments for boiler systems in hospitals, department stores.

Big systems. I was out there selling for him. I got a second job working as a waiter at Friday's in Sheepshead Bay. We needed the money. The restaurant would close at something like 1:00, 2:00 in the morning, and then people would hang around and drink for a couple of hours after closing. I wasn't getting home until very late. There were a couple of times when I didn't get home until the sun was already up. Danielle had had enough; I had had enough. We were at a family bar mitzvah when I got my wife, my parents, and everybody together and said to them, "Look, I need help." I was the one who initiated the conversation that day. It was inevitable. I was putting Danielle through hell, not coming home, all kinds of shit. It was terrible.

The 30 days in Wernersville seemed like an eternity. It seemed like 1,000 days. My wife was back in New York, and I had been married for only three years. I didn't even have a career at the time. I didn't have any direction, we didn't have any kids, didn't have a house, didn't have anything. When I left that day, I didn't know if I would ever see my wife again because I had put her through hell in those first three years of marriage. I didn't know if she was going to stick around when I went away to rehab, but she did.

At the time it was worthwhile. After rehab was over they said to me, *You can't go back to where you were, because of people, places, and things. Your old haunts and old friends and all the people you knew when you were using are going to be around there. It's going to put you right back where you were before you got here.* They recommended I go to a halfway house. For someone who had abused drugs for 10 years, 30 days in a rehab isn't going to cut it. They asked me where I'd like to live outside of New York. I told them, "Florida. I went to college down there, and my parents have a condominium down there. It's my second home."

I went to a place called the Boca House, a halfway house in Boca Raton. I lived with other people who were addicts. There were four guys in every apartment, all of us addicts. Usually you go to work during the day, and typically the jobs were pretty humiliating. No one in these places was trading stocks, you know? I got down there in the summer, and I spent days in a shirt and tie in 90-degree heat. I didn't have a car and spent my days walking up and down Federal Highway in Florida trying to find myself some type of job. I got a job at Marshall's department store as a cashier, making about $70 a week. Other guys were working in gas stations. We worked during the day, and at night we went to meetings. Ninety meetings in 90 days, and you don't see your family in the first couple of weeks. Eventually they can come down to visit on the weekends. Danielle was in New York, and she came back and forth to visit me. Ultimately, Danielle moved to Florida, and we set up shop down there and started a life.

I went into it because I wanted to. I wasn't doing it because I got arrested or because someone made me do it. I spent three months at the halfway house. I spent a long time in sobriety, going to meetings. I got a job at CBS SportsLine. Honestly, drugs and drinking didn't come back again for the most part until I was working in radio.

The first time I used again was in 1998. I was in San Diego for the Super Bowl. The Packers were playing the Broncos, Brett Favre against John Elway. I was there for something like 10 days, and that's when I started to dabble again. My MO was that once I went to rehab, it wasn't going to happen in front of my wife again. I wasn't going to do it in Florida. I wasn't going to come home after being out all night. If I was away for the Super Bowl for eight days or for the Pro Bowl or something like that, that's usually when I got into trouble. When I was away from home and in settings where there were parties, I couldn't help myself. Then we went to New York, I got the job at WNEW in 2000, and it was still kind of the same thing.

The one that everybody remembers, the one that really sent me over the edge, happened in Cleveland. I was covering a fight, Butterbean Esch fought that night, and football players Michael Westbrook fought Jarrod Bunch. Pay-Per-View TV paid me good money to cover the fight. I was in the ring after every fight to interview the winners and losers. It was fun. It was a cold, snowy night in Cleveland, and I was staying in a hotel that was near Cleveland State. When the fights were over, a bunch of people from the crowd went down to a section in Cleveland called the Flats, a big bar district. I partied there for about two fucking days.

It had been a pretty bad stretch for me. Eight or nine months before then, I had been partying at the Republican National Convention in September 2004. And then came the Super Bowl in Jacksonville in January 2005. So, when I got to Cleveland in February 2005, I had already been into it. My daughter Ava was 10 months old at the time. I carried around a picture of her; it was like a director's cut frame with a picture in it. It was a Sunday, and I was really, really having a tough time. Quite frankly, I was suicidal. I was in Cleveland, I was fucked up for two straight days, my wife and daughter were home. I knew at that point it was time to either go to rehab and get my life in order, or it was going to be a mess. I contemplated suicide that day. I took the picture of Ava out of my pocket. I was shaken. It wasn't like I saw her picture that day and then I went clean because I fucked up soon enough. In September 2005 I went to Atlantic City and lost my job at FAN for good. I won't say that that moment turned my life around and that afterward I was a complete angel. But it was the first time (maybe the second time if you count the night when she was born) where the power of loving your kid was enough to save me in the moment. If I hadn't seen Ava's picture that morning, I might have jumped from the 14th floor of the Marriott Hotel in Cleveland.

I came home and said to my wife, "Here we go again." She was shocked. I told her I'd really been struggling lately on some of these trips and that I needed to go away again. She was very supportive, as she's always been.

I didn't want to travel again because I had a baby now. I didn't want to be in a different state. When I went to Mark Chernoff and Lee Davis at FAN, they were great. They told me, "Go away, take care of yourself and your family, and when you come back in 30 days, your job will be waiting for you." I was surprised. I wasn't sure it was going to go that way. But the FAN was behind me. They were totally supportive, and I knew that when I got out of rehab I was going to get my job back with Imus and with Joe Benigno.

I wanted to stay local, and heard about a place in New Jersey that was supposed to be great, a place called Sunrise House in Lafayette. I was living in Tenafly, New Jersey, at the time. The problem was, they had no beds available. The place was packed. Luckily, somebody relatively famous who had gone to Sunrise House before I had was willing to make a call on my behalf. That somebody was Lawrence Taylor. He called and got me a bed. When I got out of rehab, I made weekly visits back, in addition to the daily AA meetings and drug counseling. I actually used Lawrence's drug counselor. I went once a week to Summit, New Jersey, to sit down with this guy. He was an older guy and a wonderful man. He is the guy who Lawrence Taylor credits with getting him on the right track. Lawrence really did a lot of the legwork for me. I knew him through my agent, Mark Lepselter; Lawrence was also his client. Lawrence had been on the air with me a couple of times at WFAN, and he loved coming on because he thought I was crazy. He knows that everyone else he goes on with has his own agenda, and all of them are full of shit. With me he just thought *That motherfucker's crazy.* We've gone out for dinners, but I've never partied with him. We didn't have that type of relationship. He knew I loved him, and there was a reason he took a liking to me. It was obvious. I had a drug problem, I was always in trouble, always in the news. I think he thought, *Hey, other than the fact I sacked the quarterback, we have a lot in common.*

It went well. I came home in March 2005, I was doing great, and got my job back at FAN. Then of course two months after that in May 2005 the Kylie Minogue incident cost me my job with Imus. Three months after that, in September, came my ill-fated trip to Atlantic City. I slipped again, and that was it. I never made it back for the Giants pregame against the Cardinals. The date was September 11. And that was it for FAN.

But I still had my family, and for that I felt very fortunate. There were guys from AA, NA, and GA whose wives and kids, mothers and fathers, and brothers and sisters had all walked away and left them all alone. That never happened to me. My wife is still with me. And my family still supports me. Has my reputation taken a hit along the way? No doubt about it. Have I lost friends and destroyed business relationships along the way? I would say so. Probably not friends—friends usually stick around. Of course, it was hard on my parents. I'm their son. They love me and they love my wife and my children, and they had to endure it all too. I try to explain to certain people that it's bad enough when you go through it as a family. I have very doting parents, to whom I am very grateful. I grew up in a very tight-knit family, my sisters and my parents and I are all very close. But because of my job, we also had to endure it through the media. In my first weekend back from rehab in 2005, my face was emblazoned in the *New York Post*, and the caption read, *Imus' Sports Guy And Crack*, or something like that. It's bad enough when your family, who loves you, sees it, but it's their daughter-in-law and their grandchildren that have to read about it in the papers, too.

I still speak to people with addictions all the time. I still go to meetings. Usually I'm a guy who people like to talk to because they know who I am. These programs are supposed to be anonymous, but anonymity can only last so long. All it takes is one person to recognize you.

Along the way certainly I've sabotaged myself. Look, I'll make it as easy as possible. If I didn't have the off-the-field issues, I know I would be the biggest radio star to work in New York. If not now, then when Mike Francesa leaves. It's not even debatable. Any job, the job that Craig Carton and Boomer Esiason got, would have been mine. I'd be working with Francesa right now. No disrespect to Joe Benigno or anybody else, but I'd be the biggest guy in New

York. End of story. I'd have all the SNY TV shows and all that shit. So I sabotaged myself a million times along the way.

I hear the same thing in Miami. Hank Goldberg retires, this guy's leaving, that guy's leaving, you stay straight Sid, and in three years you'll be the biggest star in the history of Miami sports talk radio. I've heard it a million times from huge people in the business. But then I've derailed myself a couple million times.

When you go into rooms for meetings, a lot of these people are down on their luck. They've lost their wives, their kids, their homes, they have nothing. And they know who you are, and they know you've had a modicum of success. I like talking to people. I think I'm a nice person; if I can help somebody I certainly will try. When you put all these things together, it's easy to see why a lot of people do come to me for advice and help. But I never tell them what to do. I've fallen off the fucking thing a million times, a million. I'm nobody's example.

Maybe Getting Loaded Before That Press Conference Wasn't a Good Idea

My FAN partner Joe Benigno and I go to a restaurant, and I have a couple of double Bloody Marys. We leave for the Knicks game, take the train, and arrive at Madison Square Garden. We're early, and I don't know what to do. Joe says to me, "Let's go into the pregame press conference." Isiah Thomas was the coach of the Knicks at the time. So I say *What the hell. I'm feeling no pain.*

We get to the press conference and go into the back of the room, where I see Mike Breen, the voice of the Knicks. I love Mike, so I sit down next to him. Benigno is standing to my left. The Knicks had just acquired Tim Thomas after he had played 42 games in Milwaukee that year. Isiah Thomas is up there at the podium extolling Thomas' virtues. He says the Knicks are excited to get Thomas because he's going to regain the form that he had before and he's going to bring a defensive presence to the team. I literally stumble to my feet and raise my hand, kind of like Arnold Horshack in *Welcome Back, Kotter*. I'm all the way in the back of the room, and there are 40 or so reporters there. Joe and I very rarely went to games together, and I very rarely went to Knicks games. And if I did go to a Knicks game or a Rangers game at MSG, I very rarely went to any press conferences. I just didn't do that. I would go to the games and talk about them the next day on the air, but I didn't go to the press conferences. To me, that was for the media. I never considered myself media, and I still don't. I'm an entertainer—not very good at it, but I'm an entertainer.

So I'm in this press conference, and I have no idea what the rules are. I don't know the etiquette of the press conference. I just kind of get up, stumble to my feet ,and say, "Isiah." He acknowledged me and I said, "Defensive presence? Regain the form? He never had the form, and he could never defend! Since when does Tim Thomas play any defense? Are you talking about the same Tim Thomas we know?"

Obviously everybody laughed—I don't think they were used to guys drunk at the press conference and then taking Isiah Thomas to task like I did. I mean everybody in the room started laughing, even Breen. Isiah even smirked, a shit-eating grin, and he actually did answer my question. It was obvious that he was annoyed. And Breen started distancing himself from me. There had been a complete lack of respect between me and Isiah.

We stayed for the game. I remember that night they were introducing Brittny and Lisa Gastineau, who were sitting right next to us. They were there to promote their TV show on E!, *Gastineau Girls* (I appeared in the first episode by the way). I remember sitting next to them and drinking. I knocked over a couple of drinks in the hallway, and at one point a security guard came over to me and said, "I'm a fan of yours and I love you, but you're getting very, very close to getting thrown out of here."

* * *

When I was on WFAN with Jody McDonald, we had the Giants' quarterback, Kerry Collins, on every Monday at 10:00 AM Mike and the Dog had the coach, and Jody McDonald and I had the quarterback. Kerry came on with us after one game in which he played horrible. The interview started, and the first thing I said was, "Kerry, I don't know how you can't take this the wrong way, but your offense has become unwatchable." The Giants had played a couple of bad games in a row.

That comment prompted Kerry's agent to call up Mark Chernoff and say, "Kerry doesn't want to do the show anymore. Sid's just disrespectful. That's not the way to talk to the guy." And that was it. It was his last time on the show. I never spoke to Kerry Collins after that. Obviously he can't stand me.

Years later I went down to Miami and did the show with Dolphins player O.J. McDuffie. O.J. was my partner when I first came down to Miami in 2005, and he and Kerry Collins are both Penn State alumni. Also, O.J.'s best friend is Ki-Jana Carter, who played with Kerry in college. Penn State was poised to win the national championship that year. They had lost one game, to Michigan, and O.J. wanted to bring on Kerry Collins to talk about the big game between Penn State and Florida State. I told him, "Just so you know, bro, he doesn't like me. We had this thing when he was with the Giants, and I don't think he's forgotten it."

O.J. said, "He'll be cool." Sure enough, Kerry came on. I said to him, "Kerry, I didn't think there would ever come a day when you and I would be talking on the radio again." He said, coolly, "Sid, I'm not here for you."

* * *

I had trashed Bobby Valentine on my show for a while. I know he got the Mets in the NLCS in 1999 and the World Series in 2000, but he had a lousy year in 2001, and it was after the 2002 season when the Mets finished last that he got fired. I was working with Jody McDonald, and we were going back and forth whether or not Bobby should be fired. By 2002 I had had enough of him. Jody Mac kept saying to me, "I'm not about to fire the guy only two years removed from the World Series," and on and on, until it became embarrassing. Every time the Mets would lose a game— they were in last place—I'd ask him, "Are you embarrassed yet? Are you embarrassed yet?" and Jody would say, "I'm not there yet." Eventually he agreed with me.

And then Bobby Valentine got fired. Bobby's out—this is after 2002—and we were discussing something about the Mets and I started ripping on Valentine. He had already been fired. He's out. I didn't know where the hell he was. I thought he might be in Japan.

The segment came to an end and somebody in the newsroom announced, "Bobby Valentine is on the phone. He wants to talk to you." I was thinking to myself, *This has to be [producer] Eddie Scozzare or somebody playing a joke. There's no way Bobby Valentine is calling me. Why would he care about me?* I picked up the phone and sure enough, it was Bobby Valentine. In my entire life, I had never heard the word "fuck" more than I did in those five minutes. If you took every episode of *The Sopranos* and added up the amount of "fucks" that were used along the way it would still come up short against Bobby in that five-minute phone call. He motherfucked me up and down, yelling, "I listened to your bullshit for years and you talk fucking bad about me? I have my 10-year-old daughter in the car, and she has to listen to your fucking bullshit about how I stabbed people in the back and I'm a bad guy? Who the fuck do you think you are? You think you know something about fuckin' baseball? You know fuckin' nothing." Fuck this, fuck this, fuck me, fuck that about 1,000 times. That was the end of that.

Ironically, he came on for a couple of shows later that year. Bobby had a hotel by Shea Stadium. Bobby sat down with me and Jody, and he was fine. It was as if it had never happened.

* * *

Larry Csonka was a fucking disaster. This is going back to my early, early days when I was doing my first radio show called *The Drive* with Scott Kaplan. It was back at the beginning of my radio career on SportsLine.com in Florida. Way back in the day we interviewed Larry Csonka. I went on and on: "Larry, you're the greatest fullback of all time.... You ran with reckless abandon. Bob Griese's in

the Hall of Fame, and Paul Warfield is in the Hall of Fame—
because of you.... I love Jim Kiick and Mercury Morris, but basically you were the whole team, and a lot of the Dolphins' success
was predicated on you."

It was a complete blow job for 15 minutes. *Complete.* At the
very end of the interview, the very last question, I said "Larry, with
all these great things you talked about, I have to ask you about this.
What the hell happened that day with Joe Pisarcik at Giants
Stadium?" Of course, I was referring to "the Fumble." I swear to
you, he didn't laugh, he didn't giggle. He said, "I will jump through
the phone—what's your name?" I said, "Sid," and he continued, "I
will jump through the phone, Sid, and I will break your nose."

I interviewed him again about eight years later. He had forgotten about it, and it was all good. But suffice it to say, I did not
bring up the Pisarcik fumble again.

* * *

After the Giants' 2002 playoff game against the 49ers, I just
destroyed Jason Sehorn on the air. And that's where our relationship ended.

I had become close with Jason. We were friendly. In fact, his
charity had a bowling event down at Chelsea Piers. He and his
wife, the beautiful Angie Harmon, actually had me host their
bowling event one year. There were all kinds of Giants, Mets, and
Yankees players there. So on the Monday after that terrible playoff
game, Jason came in to the show. I asked him, "Hey Jason, what the
fuck was that yesterday with Terrell Owens in the fourth quarter?"
And then he pulled what for me is the cardinal radio sin. He said,
"How many times have you had to cover T.O.?" I don't want to
talk to any athlete who ever says that to me. Fuck you—that's not
my job, thank you very much. It got nasty and it got ugly, and I
didn't talk to Jason for years.

Then in 2008, it just so happened that I went to OPEN Sports
with Mike Levy, and Jason Sehorn was one of the athletes they

hired to do weekly blogs and come on my video show. So I did speak to Jason a couple of times. I brought up the incident, and we agreed to bury the hatchet. But for years Jason was another athlete who couldn't stand me.

* * *

Randy Shannon, the head football coach of the Miami Hurricanes, appeared on my show once—and only once. Larry Coker had been the head coach at Miami for a long time and had enjoyed a lot of early success. The Hurricanes won a championship in 2001 and should have won another, but they got screwed on a bad interference call against Ohio State. So in actuality Coker was really a pubic hair away from winning two national championships. But by the time he was done, Miami had really fallen apart.

So into this mess walked Randy Shannon, and he agreed to come on my show. I went to Miami, though I didn't graduate from there. I'll be the first to admit I was a bit combative. Shannon had played for Miami; he was a linebacker on teams that won national championships. He was a defensive coordinator for Larry Coker, and everybody else got fired from Coker's staff except for Shannon, who was named the head coach. It seemed like the right move. The defense had always been good under Coker, even when they weren't winning. The fact he's an African American and that he had a great relationship with the local high schools such as Northwestern and St. Thomas Aquinas was also a plus. I could see why it made sense to bring him in despite the fact he had no head coaching experience.

So he came on the air, and I immediately started peppering him. "Who's the quarterback?" He can't tell me yet. At the time it was a battle between Kyle Wright and Kirby Freeman, and both of them sucked. I was like, "What about this offense, Randy? Are you going to score points?" He said to me, "What kind of question is that? What do you expect me to tell you, we're not?" I said, "If you are, how are you going to do it? The last two years you haven't been able to do it. Tell me this running back is going to have a big year. Tell me this wide receiver is going to have a big year. Give me specific reasons why this offense is going to score points, because I don't see it."

He was upset. He thought that I was just being combative and disrespectful, and he told Mark Pray, the athletics director, he would never go on my show again. I have not spoken to the guy since that time.

WE NOW INTERRUPT OUR REGULARLY SCHEDULED BROADCAST
FOR A WORD FROM...

JIM NANTZ, CBS Sports

I first really ran across Sid in 1998. He was partnering with Scott Kaplan on a sports call-in show that was really ahead of its time. It was on CBS SportsLine, and it was an Internet-based show. It did not have a radio home.

It didn't take a talent scout to figure out these two both were very gifted individuals. They knew how to make a show interesting. You could tell that right away. I remember one time, I don't know why, I was at the Final Four in San Antonio in 1998. Tubby Smith would eventually win it, and they were out there doing shows for CBS SportsLine. The day of the championship game, that Monday, I invited them to come up to my room to hang out. I was getting ready to go to the game, and they came up and just chatted for a little bit. They were a lot of fun to hang out with. Sid helped me pick out some socks. I was putting an outfit out that I was going to wear that night. I don't know what the punchline is to that. He made a big to-do about that on the air. He felt a tremendous pride of ownership that they were somehow involved in what socks I wore that night on the national championship game. I think it was more the color of the socks. I'm a bit colorblind, so the boys came up and helped me.

I wish he was in New York. I think he belongs in the New York market. I really believe he's got a vibe for the New York sports fan's mind-set. He really thinks like a New Yorker does. After all, he is one. I'm glad he's got a new deal at a great radio station in Miami, but it baffles me that he's kept out of the New York market right now. I just think he would have a following wherever he would end up. But there are certain things people can't get past.

He's unfiltered, which is something that is going to bring whatever you want to call it—great radio, provocative comments, controversy. He doesn't have these little editors hanging out in his brain. If he thinks of something that is pure genius, he just instantly releases it. It comes right out of the chute and comes right out of his mouth. Sid, to best describe him, is unfiltered, but he is extremely lovable and kind-hearted. It's an interesting dynamic there. I'm not a psychologist, so I don't know what the terms would be, but sometimes I think it's all triggered by an insecurity deep inside: people like him know this unfiltered side of them is really creative and interesting and provocative, but that's not really what's in their heart. He has a big heart. I've talked to Sid a lot off the air, and even though he can be controversial and he can drive the truck into a wall with his commentary, he's not really one to hurt anybody. I miss him. I did go on his show. I wish it was more often, but I just can't always schedule it. I really thought he and [Mike] Francesa would have been a really good team.

I do consider him a friend. His dad had an episode this summer, and he was freaking out over it. He texted me. He was so, so worried—and rightfully so. That's the real Sid. That's who he is. I could totally feel what he was going through. He's made a lot of allusions to my book, *Always by My Side*, really hitting home with him because of his own relationship with his dad. I think he really gets it now. Sid's been through a lot in his life, and his dad's been his rock and his inspiration. You can really tell Sid seeks his dad's love and approval. I was feeling for him. The first reports coming out from him sure didn't sound very positive. Sid was teetering on desperation. I'm just so thankful that his dad rallied.

Sometimes being on the *Imus* show I think he felt a certain freedom that the parameters of what's accepted and what's not even got a little wider, a little broader. There was room for him to explore the craziness a little bit more. I'm sure he felt that. Of course, the world has changed since then, and it's not only changed for Sid, it changed for Don. You can tell Don was really smitten by him. I think that was one of the great validating moments of Sid's career. Here's a guy who has seen it all, done it all, who has had tremendous lasting power in the business. And you can just hear it in his voice—the way he involved Sid in his show, he saw someone with talent. In some ways I'm sure Don saw a young Don Imus in Sid, a guy that reminded him a lot of himself, the next generation, the modern-day version of the young Don Imus. I think Don really recognizes Sid's talent. I've always taken that as a sign of true validation for Sid's abilities.

How a Jewish Kid Growing Up in Brooklyn Met the Mets

My dad used to get his hair cut in Brooklyn by this guy named Joe. Joe the barber had a place on Avenue U in Brooklyn. In October 1973 I was six years old. I distinctly remember walking into the barber shop and looking into the back of the shop. There were always a couple of guys in there hanging out and smoking cigars. They had lollipops for the kids, and they always had the ballgame on the radio. It was a scene reminiscent of the movie *A Bronx Tale*, when Little C would walk into the bar and all the guys would be in there shooting dice and talking sports. That movie could just as well depicted Brooklyn in the 1970s. I love that movie; it's one of my all-time favorites.

So anyway, that's what it was like. I was like Little C going to get a hair cut with my dad. I don't know why, but I distinctly remember the radio: Wayne Garrett was at the plate for the Mets, and he was facing Vida Blue. It was the 1973 World Series against the A's. As it turned out, Garrett hit a home run that day. It was Game 5. The Mets, playing behind Jerry Koosman, beat Vida Blue. Tug McGraw got the save, and they won 2–0 and went up three games to two. Then, of course, Tom Seaver lost to Catfish Hunter in Game 6, Jon Matlack lost to Ken Holtzman in Game 7, when Bert Campaneris and Reggie Jackson hit home runs. But I was hooked. I became a die-hard Mets fan after that.

My father grew up in a Brooklyn Dodgers household. As a little boy, he was a Brooklyn Dodgers fan. My grandfather was a Brooklyn Dodgers fan. There were no Yankees fans in my lineage and no New York Giants fans either. They were all Brooklyn Dodger fans. The Dodgers and the Giants both left after the 1957 season, and those fans had to wait around for five years until the Mets came around in 1962. Part of the beauty of that 1973 Mets team, my first sports memory, was good and bad. Willie Mays came back to play for the Mets in '72 and '73. At that point in his career he was pretty pathetic—he hit only 14 home runs with the Mets, hit about .230 combined, missed balls in the outfield, and so on. He was a shell of what he used to be when he played for the New York Giants, obviously, and the San Francisco Giants. But he was still Willie Mays. And that was the beginning of my Mets fandom.

I remember the Mets trading Seaver like it was yesterday. How could I predict that later on in life I would work with Jody McDonald, who was my co-host on the FAN for a couple of years. Jody's father, Joe McDonald, was the GM of the Mets and the guy who traded Tom Seaver. Now, I'm not sure it was his call—I think it was M. Donald Grant and the owners of the Mets who wanted to make the trade—but in the end it was Joe McDonald who traded Seaver in the middle of the 1977 season. That was a killer for me. I was only 10 years old at the time, and of course he was my favorite player. He was 7–3 with the Mets, and he went 14–3 with Cincinnati to end the year 21–6. It was a crushing moment in my Mets fandom when Jody's father traded Seaver to the Reds for Pat Zachry, Doug Flynn, Steve Henderson, and Dan Norman.

My next-door neighbor was a kid by the name of Joseph Iovine. He was my best friend growing up. I idolized him. He was good-looking, Italian, and drove a Pontiac Firebird back then. He worked out, all the girls loved him, his father was a good-looking and prominent Brooklyn attorney. They lived very, very nicely and he was *the man*. It was very similar to the John Travolta character in

Saturday Night Fever. People would just look at him like, "He's the man." That was kind of how I felt about Joseph. To me, he was larger than life. (As it turned out, he would later introduce me to some of the things that would get me into trouble down the road. In our adolescent years, the first time I went out and partied in the city and did a bunch of different things, it was with Joseph.)

Our families were very, very close. My family trusted him. They trusted us, and he was a die-hard Mets fan. In the football season we didn't do much together because he was a Dolphins fan. He became a bigger Dolphins fan when Dan Marino came along, because he was the king of the Italians.

We used to play two games together all the time, growing up between 1973 and 1977. One was Shortstop-to-First, where I would take a tennis ball, stand by my mother's garage, Joseph would stand at the end of the driveway, and we would throw each other ground balls. Every time you fielded it cleanly and threw it back to the other guy that was an out. If you missed it, it was a single, a double, or triple, depending on how badly you missed it.

The other game we played was dice baseball. I remember playing Strat-o-Matic baseball later on in life; dice baseball was the same thing. Joseph and I would put together index cards of all the players and put the lineups down. If you rolled a two it was a home run, if you rolled a three it was a triple, and if you rolled a four it was an out. We spent hours and hours and hours playing Shortstop-to-First and dice baseball. We played all day, every day leading up to the Mets game. When the Mets game started it was huge for us. That's all we cared about, playing this game with a tennis ball and dice baseball. We kept the statistics for our dice baseball game, every single number. It was *the* most important thing to Joseph and me. Later on in life we went out to clubs and chased girls and did drugs, but at that point in our lives it was all about the Mets. And boy, were they horrible. But it didn't matter. We loved the Mets, and that was it.

The two of us probably watched 100 Mets games together each year. We were young kids, and our dads worked late. We went into Joseph's basement—he lived right next door to me in Brooklyn on Quentin Road—put the air conditioning on, and turned on the game. His mom would order us a pizza, and we'd watch the Mets game every single night. We did that for years.

After Seaver was gone my favorite player was Lee Mazzilli. It was obvious why: Maz was a Brooklyn kid, he went to Lincoln High School, and every once in a while you'd see him at Wheeler's in Sheepshead Bay. Here's a Brooklyn kid, a really good-looking guy. It was funny, I used to always argue back and forth as a kid with the Islanders/Rangers fans and the Jets/Giants fans about Phil Simms and Richard Todd, Bryan Trottier, and Ron Duguay. The one argument we had back then was who was better looking, Lee Mazzilli or Bucky Dent? Who got more chicks, Maz or Dent?

It was before the 1981 baseball season and we were headed to Florida, like we did every year. This was the year I was finally going to have the chance to go to spring training and meet Lee Mazzilli and Dave Kingman. The Mets had John Stearns, Hubie Brooks, Lee Mazzilli, and a very young Mookie Wilson. They even had Ellis Valentine, one of the worst trades in Mets history, by the way, whom they had gotten in exchange for Jeff Reardon.

I was there at spring training in the hopes of meeting Maz and Dave Kingman. Mazzilli walked out, and he had more bodyguards than the president. Kingman walked out with his flannel shirt and jeans and it was obvious, he fucking hated everybody. This was the guy who once sent a rat's head to the media. He didn't like kids; he didn't like anybody. Kingman was one of the surliest bastards ever. Maz came out like he was Mr. Movie Star. And I came home that day with one signature: a guy I never heard of, who ended up that year as the backup shortstop, getting 48 at-bats. My luck, the guy is now more famous because he's the manager of the Minnesota Twins: Ron Gardenhire. His was the only signature I got that day. That turned me off to Maz and

Kingman and the Mets a little bit. But they were so terrible at that point it didn't really matter.

Mookie was always close to my heart. The name was just totally cool. It was just a funny name. It's as simple as that. Plus, he was exciting to watch. He stole bases. We just fell in love with the guy right away. Joe and I kept statistics for our dice baseball league. We used an old black-and-white composition notebook. On the front of the notebook it read, "The Mookie Book."

Wilson was just a home-grown guy, and for years I had no idea what his name meant. Later on I found out that his real name is William Wilson and that when he was a baby he couldn't say the word "milk" so he asked his grandmother, "More mook, more mook." So they called him Mookie. He was a likeable guy with a great smile—he always smiling on his baseball card. He just became *the guy*. He was there before Keith Hernandez and Gary Carter and Darryl Strawberry and all those guys. When he was there, there weren't a lot of Mets players to love. (Then of course, he was involved in probably the greatest play ever, in 1986, as a New York Mets fan. You know, the one with Bill Buckner.) Early on in my FAN career I once said it is tough being a Mets fan, because the Yankees have the House That Ruth Built and we've got the House That Mookie Built.

And then of course the great years came after that. Strawberry came up in '83, and he won the Rookie of the Year Award and hit 26 homers. Then in 1984, they got Keith Hernandez and the next year, Gary Carter, and the rest is history. I was back in Brooklyn, attending Kingsborough Community College at that point. I had left in 1984 for college, but that didn't last very long. I was home in three months, actually. It was a disaster. I developed a great tennis game and a heinous cocaine problem. At any rate, Strawberry fast became my favorite player. To this day he is my favorite Met of all time.

The one thing I will say about Davey Johnson with the Mets— and I told this to him, right to his face— is that as great as it was to win it in '86, I really thought that team was a tremendous disappointment. They were so talented, they should have won more than one. In 1987 they picked up Kevin McReynolds and traded Kevin Mitchell. I thought for sure that '87 team was going to win the World Series. And then they ran into Orel Hershiser, who had 90 straight scoreless innings or some ridiculous streak going, and he broke Don Drysdale's record. The only guy who could touch him was Gregg Jefferies, who was a rookie. The Mets lost the NLCS on Mike Scioscia's home run off Dwight Gooden. That fucking killed me. Then it all started to fall apart.

There were the horrible teams of the '90s with Saberhagen and Bobby Bonilla and Jeff Torborg and Dallas Green. There were some really rough years, and then the Mets became good again. I started radio in 1997, and that's when the Mets started to improve. That's when they got Mike Piazza.

Mark Chernoff is probably going to kill me for this, but it is what it is. It was a frustrating relationship at FAN with the Mets because Jody McDonald and I were the first midday team, and Jody of course was a Mets guy since his dad was the former GM of the team. Then they had me and Joe Benigno, the biggest Mets fans on earth. In the afternoons were Mike and Chris. I have all the respect in the world for both those guys. I love Francesa to death and I think Russo's just a little bit of a phony, but I understood what they were and what they meant to the industry. I was okay with all that. But there were times when I got frustrated, when I thought, *Hey, you know what, how about throwing us a bone once in a while?*

Mike is a die-hard Yankees fan and Chris Russo is a die-hard San Francisco Giants fan who hates the Mets, by the way. Joe and I were doing middays, and we are both die-hard Mets fans. We had a great relationship with the Mets, but we never got to talk to Bobby Valentine; we never got Art Howe. The only time I ever spoke to those guys is when I filled in for Mike and the Mad Dog over the summer. Meanwhile, those guys got Tom Glavine and

Piazza and all the great Mets players for years and years. We didn't have a Mets player who came on every single week. Every time I went to the PR guy, Jay Horwitz, and asked for a big-time Mets player, it was like, "Well, Mike and Chris are getting them, so you'll take Joe McEwing or Steve Trachsel." They got Al Leiter or Mike Hampton and we got Steve Trachsel. I was at the flagship for the Mets but that midday show was always the stepchild. *We* were the big Mets fans, but we never really got the Mets' respect because of our time slot.

I never felt like a second-class citizen because I'm a Mets fan. It's one thing to be a New Jersey Nets fan. If you're a Nets fan, you're a second-class citizen because the Knicks own that city. If you're a New York Islanders fan, despite the fact they won four Stanley Cups in the '80s, you're a second-class citizen to the Rangers. People talk about the Mets being around since just 1962, but I don't look at it that way. As far as I'm concerned, the Mets are an extension of the Brooklyn Dodgers and the New York Giants. I know the Mets came along in 1962 and they sucked, but to me those other teams have been there forever.

I'm fully aware the Yankees have 27 world championships. I'm fully aware that they spend the most money, and I'm also fully aware that, specifically in the George Steinbrenner era, the Yankees get the back page of the sports section 9 out of 10 times. I'm fully aware of that. But to me the Mets are not like the Nets or the Islanders. The Mets are kind of right there. We've had some exciting moments, like winning the World Series in 1986. It didn't help in 2000—that was frustrating, losing to the Yankees in what wasn't even really a close series. I will say this—and I've said this to my family as well—being a Yankees fan has to be boring, and frustrating. It's boring on one hand because they've won 27 world championships. So when they win a World Series, it's kind of been there, done that. The other extreme is you have to be really frustrated when your team is spending about $200 million a year and they lose in the World Series to Arizona in

2001 and in 2003 to the Marlins, of all teams. Or worse, they don't make it at all.

As a Mets fan you don't expect to win the World Series. I know the Mets usually have the second-or-third highest payroll, up there with the Dodgers or the Red Sox, but the expectation to win a World Series is not there. It's not the same sense of entitlement that one has as a Yankees fan. To me, you build more character with a team like the Mets, because they are up and down. They're not exactly the black sheep, but they're also not exactly the favorite son, either. Which is why I relate to them; the Mets are kind of like me. You root for 'em, you love 'em, but they tend to disappoint every now and then. They're never going to be the big dog in that city, but you love 'em anyway. To me, Mets fans have more character than Yankees fans. It's too easy being a Yankees fan.

Oy Vey

I went to a private school, Poly Prep in Brooklyn, until the 10th grade, after which I transferred to Solomon Schechter High School on Church Avenue and East 5th, right by the entrance of the Prospect Expressway. Poly Prep was a lot of money—a lot of money. I mean, I'm talking like college tuition–level money. I wasn't doing well there. I was hanging out with a bunch of kids that were leading me in the wrong direction, if you will. My parents were spending a lot of money to send me there, and they were like, "Fuck this." So they decided, "Hey, you know what? Put him with a bunch of Jews in a Yeshiva. Let's see if he turns his life around."

Schechter is mainly a conservative Jewish school, but there were plenty of Orthodox kids in there, too. I was in 12th grade in high school and I had half my day in Hebrew and the other half English. I had Talmud and Chumash classes. My parents sent me there because I was hanging out with a lot of Italians and getting into trouble at Poly Prep. The old "He's Jewish, put him with the Jewish kids, put him with the kids who were going to stay out of trouble" philosophy didn't quite ring true, unfortunately. There was more trouble at Schechter with drugs and gambling than there was at my previous school. These guys who wore *yarmulkes* and *tzitzis* all day—these guys were fucking maniacs. My drug-taking and gambling days got a lot worse at Solomon Schechter. A lot worse. Half my class did blow. Some of these kids, the Israelis and kids who spoke Hebrew—trust me, put 'em out on a weekend and forget it.

I'll never forget my senior trip at Solomon Schechter. We had raised money for the yearbook. Everybody was putting in money. I was the president of the student council, and the council treasurer and I decided to take all that money for the yearbook, and buy drugs to take down to Florida with us. The yearbook was supposed to be something like 300 pages, and it was something like 20—I swear to God. We had these grand plans for this amazing yearbook and it turned out everybody had their own page, there was a little collage of pictures, and that was it. The yearbook literally got cut to shreds because we took all the money and spent it on drugs for our senior trip. We stayed at a place called the Five Coins Inn in the Galt Ocean Mile section of Fort Lauderdale, and we partied like maniacs in Yesterday's and Christopher's. My parents took me out of Poly Prep because they were spending $5,000 for me to get no grades and hang out with a bunch of mobster kids. The Jewish kids in the Yeshiva, they made it 10 times worse. Less money, more *tsuris*.

My religion back then was cocaine and sports. You can put a book in front of me right now and I can read Hebrew like a fucking rabbi, I'm great at it. I was a halfway decent student and I was class president and played basketball and softball. And with my extra curricular activities I was as good as it got. I did my homework and got my grades and ended getting a scholarship to the University Miami. But by that time I was already going out in the city and doing drugs; I was already in trouble. *Send him to Yeshiva for a couple of years. That will straighten him out. Keep him with the nice Jewish kids.* Well, most of the kids at Schechter were observant so they couldn't go out on Friday night, but you get them after shabbos on Saturday night, and they're fucking animals.

I remember one kid; he lived downstairs and his parents lived upstairs. He was a shabbos observer. I was going out on Friday nights in the city, and I would meet him downstairs during shabbos. He would do a couple of quick bumps of blow with me, and I'd leave and go out into the city for the night. I'd hear from him again the next night. He'd still be up from the night before, never gone to bed. He went to shul the next morning all wired off his fucking face to do his *minyan* thing. When he met me out on Saturday night, he had already been up for 24 hours. That Solomon Schechter of Brooklyn is actually out of business now. It's defunct. I wonder why.

Why I Have Charley Winner to Thank for a Lifelong Devotion to the New York Giants

With New York fans, usually it's Mets and Jets. I'm Knicks, Rangers, Giants, Mets. So why aren't I Mets and Jets like everybody else?

The answer is, I *was* Mets and Jets. I grew up a die-hard Jets fan. I had the letterman jacket like Fred Savage did in *The Wonder Years*. I had all that stuff. Joe Namath was my absolute hero. I was a little boy and my dad and I were in the A&S Department Store in New York City. They had this thing on the counter. You put your name in it, and they were going to pick a name. If they picked your name, you were going to be the mascot for the New York Jets. So of course we put my name in, thinking, *C'mon, what were the odds of that, a million kids walking around Manhattan, a million kids put their name in that box.* We put it in and totally forgot about it. Would you believe, they picked us! They picked my name out of the box, and I was going to be the mascot for the New York Jets. I was going to sit on the bench on a game day with the New York Jets players.

Of course, I was excited, but all I could think about was, *Oh my God, here's my chance to meet my childhood heroes, Joe Namath, Emerson Boozer, and all these guys I grew up with and loved dearly.* It was 1974, and I was seven years old. It was the year that Charley Winner took over for Weeb Ewbank. Charley Winner, for people who don't know or are too young, was Weeb Ewbank's son-in-law.

When Weeb left after 1973, Charley Winner took over as head coach. Namath was still there, Boozer was still there, and John Riggins was on that football team. I loved him. Guys like him and Jerome Barkum, and Rich Caster were my favorite players. I was supposed to sit on the bench for a game—it was the October 27 game against the Rams, Week 7. The problem is, after beating the Bears in Week 2, they went on to lose to Buffalo, Miami, New England, and Baltimore. So by the time the Rams game came along, the Jets were 1–5 and riding a four-game losing streak. Charley Winner decided the young kid on the sideline was going to be a distraction. He decided that little Sid Rosenberg, who was seven years old, was going to be a distraction to the Jets. The Jets called my house and got two footballs that were signed by every single player, Namath, Riggins, Boozer, all of 'em, and sent it to my house. They gave me tickets to a game, too. But I couldn't sit on the bench.

It was one of the biggest disappointments of my whole life. That was the day I became a die-hard Giants fan. We still had tickets for the Jets at Shea Stadium, so my dad would still take me, but I became a Giants fan because of what the Jets did to me. I've have since worked with Joe Namath when I worked at CBS SportsLine—Joe Namath was one of the original investors at CBS SportsLine—and I have told him that story many, many times. He basically said to me, "I don't blame ya."

In 1974, the Giants were coached by Bill Arnsparger and were 2–12. So it wasn't like I was going to a great deal. They did actually improve in 1975, my first full season as a Giants fan, to 5–9. That's what I remember, rooting for the Giants and guys like Doug Kotar and Craig Morton.

In the late '70s, when guys like Joe Pisarcik, Jerry Golsteyn, and Randy Dean were the quarterbacks of the Giants, that's when I really started to get into them. I remember very vividly when Pisarcik fumbled against the Eagles in that game in 1978. I was at a birthday party at my cousin Stephen Dehrman's house out in

New Jersey. I'll never forget it. Then Phil Simms came in '79. That team I remember like it was yesterday: Billy Taylor, Doug Kotar, Emery Moorehead, and Gary Shirk, still one of my favorite tight ends in the history of the Giants. Of course, they had great linebackers back then: Brad Van Pelt and Harry Carson and Brian Kelley. That's when I really became a Giants fan.

The first time I got really excited as a football fan was in 1981, when the Giants beat the Eagles in the playoffs. They were 9–7 in the regular season, Ray Perkins was the coach, and they beat the Eagles in the playoffs. They went on to lose a tough game to the 49ers in the divisional playoff game. Scott Brunner took over for Phil Simms because Simms got hurt that year, and I became a huge Scott Brunner fan. But I was a *huge* Rob Carpenter fan. He was the first Giant I really, really loved on offense. I loved Taylor and Carson and Van Pelt and Kelly and all those guys on defense. But Rob Carpenter, I love that guy.

I struggled about whether or not I wanted Scott Brunner or Phil Simms at quarterback. As far as media people go, Phil Simms to this day is one of my best friends. I love Phil Simms and he loves me, but I admitted that to him. It turns out that Bill Parcells was dealing with the exact same struggle. When Parcells took over for Perkins, he thought Brunner was the better quarterback. That made Giants fans crazy. At 14 or 15, I kind of felt the same way. Of course, we all came to realize that was just ridiculous.

I started going to a lot of games in 1984 and '85, with my dad and his buddies Sal Ferragamo and Richie Rotundo. The four of us were always there. Sometimes we had six or seven people, including my other brother-in-law, Albert Baker, who would come, or my brother-in-law Harry Wagowski. But our foursome was always there. We were nutty fans, real passionate, never missed a game, never missed a down.

At Poly Prep, arguments erupted between the Jets fans and the Giants fans all the time. People talked about Richard Todd and Ken O'Brien, and I'd talk about Phil Simms. I was a crazy, crazy fan. I remember the night the Mets won the World Series, when they beat the Red Sox and came back from a 3–0 deficit to win Game 7 of the 1986 World Series. I came home from school that day excited because the Mets had a chance to win the World Series, but it was also a Monday, and that night the Giants were playing the Redskins. I remember telling my father that I wanted to watch the Mets win the World Series, but I didn't want to miss the Giants and Redskins. My father had this nine-inch black-and-white TV in the kitchen. The biggest TV at the time was in the basement. So we had the big TV with the Mets and Red Sox, and we brought down the small nine-inch black-and-white from the kitchen and tuned in to the Giants and the Redskins. The Giants won that night, and it was a big win for the them. Lawrence Taylor had three sacks that night.

As a Giants fan, it was the ultimate thrill to be on the station that carried the games. Doing the pregame show for the Giants was like a dream come true. I started in 2002 and I did it for three years. I was all set to do it my fourth consecutive year in 2005, but I didn't show up for the first game of that season, Giants-Cardinals. Career at the FAN: over.

They put up a big tent and a big stage outside of Gate D at Giants Stadium, and we had a great turnout every single week. Bob Papa would come down and do a segment with me called "Name that Giant," which was kind of like *Name that Tune.* The fans would get really involved. Dave Jennings would come down. It was the ultimate thrill of my career. Would I say the most rewarding? No, obviously *Imus* was more rewarding. But to know that on a Sunday morning I could put on my Giants jersey and my red sweatpants just like 70,000 other fans, and show up at the stadium and to actually sit up on stage and have Giants fans watching me interview all these guys? That was really amazing.

Sometimes Troy Aikman would come on if it was a Fox game. Frank Gifford, all the great Giants stopped by. Carl Banks did the pregame show with me. To sit up there on stage and represent all these Giants fans was just an incredible feeling. Sunday mornings to me were as good as it got. It was the ultimate thrill. And the fans just ate it up, man.

They knew we were going to be out in front of Gate D. We went on air at 11:30 AM after Mike Francesa finished up his *NFL Now* show. It was a great lead-in. *NFL Now* has been the No. 1 show on Sunday mornings in New York for 100 years. So at the bottom of his show, it's, "Let's send it out to Sid Rosenberg out at Giants Stadium." They were packed in! People knew to stand outside of Gate D, so by the time I got on the air, I already had the crowd whooped up. We threw footballs and T-shirts out there, and they were ready to rock and roll. I would say, without sounding arrogant or obnoxious, that I was by far the best they've ever had in the pregame show. By far.

Nine times out of 10 I went inside to watch the game. Mind you, I never, ever sat in the press box even though I was doing the pregame show for the FAN. I went to my father's seats, which was another cool thing. I would do the pregame show and then walk in the stadium and take the escalator all the way upstairs, because my dad's seats were in Section 345. As I walked through the stadium to get to my seat, every two seconds there would be a high-five and a slap on the ass and a "What a great job on the pregame show. We're going to kill this team today." Giants fans were really, really receptive. By the time I sat down in my seat I was exhausted. It literally took me half an hour to get to my seat. I felt like I was playing on the team. Many a Monday morning I would come in, and I would have half a voice because I was yelling and screaming up there in Section 345 at Giants Stadium. It wasn't like I got there and I had to calm down because I'm working in the media. That was never me. I went up there and went nuts.

My dad was a Giants fan pretty much his whole life, going back to the days of Frank Gifford and all those championship teams. For him it was great. He was always one of the first ones there for the pregame show. When I sat down and got ready to do the show, I'd always see my father out there, usually him and Sal or Richie. That part really made it rough on the day I didn't show up, knowing my dad was there, like he was every time I was on the air. I don't think he missed a game in the three years I did the pregame show. He was there that morning and Mark Chernoff said to my father "Where's Sid?" And he had no idea. I never showed up. That made it doubly difficult.

But before that day, my father ate it up. There he was, a Giants fan since the days of Frank Gifford, Andy Robustelli, Y.A. Tittle, Homer Jones, and Del Shofner, all those guys. And then 20, 30 years later, his son is up there kind of leading the charge. He was very, very proud. The fact he could show up in his Giants regalia and root for the team and have me up there at the same time, it was an incredible family experience for all of us.

When the Giants shocked the Patriots in Super Bowl XLII, it was a little different for me. In 2004 Tom Coughlin took over for Jim Fassel, and I was gone in 2005. I only had one year of covering the Giants in training camp in Albany when Coughlin was there, and I didn't like him. I had made it very, very clear on the radio. I knew Wellington Mara's dying wish was to bring Coughlin in. I understood that. But I also know that Ernie Accorsi didn't want him. He wanted Romeo Crennel or Charley Weis. Wellington Mara's dying wish was to have that drill sergeant back. He wanted that Bill Parcells type back. Coughlin was there even though a lot of the guys on the Giants didn't want him. Tiki Barber hated his guts; Michael Strahan hated his guts. They all hated his guts until they fucking won. Then they won a Super Bowl, and all of a sudden everyone loves him. Jim Fassel had been so friendly with me. He was the guy I covered for a couple of years on the FAN before Coughlin. The difference between covering Fassel and then Coughlin was like night and day. I understand that Coughlin has calmed down a lot from how he was years ago, but that first summer he was a total dick. He was just businesslike. He didn't look at me during the interviews. He just kind of looked down and did his thing, as if he didn't want to be there. And then I was gone by 2005, so the rest is history.

WE NOW INTERRUPT OUR REGULARLY SCHEDULED BROADCAST FOR A WORD FROM...

TIKI BARBER, Former Giants running back, NBC correspondent

I appreciated the guys who had the knowledge. The Giants would tell me that I needed to call whoever, I needed to talk to whoever, and I would. When I worked with the FAN, I got to know some of those guys on a personal level. It was early in my career, and I was doing overnights. Every now and then I'd go into the studio during the day, and Mike and Chris were there, Steve Sommers was there, Russ Salzberg was there. All the guys on that station, their knowledge always impressed me. Their opinions didn't always impress me, but their knowledge always did.

I always felt that Sid was fair with his criticism. He wasn't just saying something to spark a discussion. I think he honestly believed in what he was saying, whereas I think some guys just say something outrageous just to say it and try to provoke a reaction from callers or athletes on what they're talking about. I never felt Sid was doing that. He's crude to the max, but that's his shtick. It's what he was asked to do and he did it very well.

I know he made that comment about the Williams sisters. In the context in which he said it, it was funny; in a vacuum it's not. That's the problem. We tend to take things that people say, take them out of the context of the entire conversation, and make them the issue. It's happened to me. If it was a Caucasian person built like the Williams sisters I think he'd say the same thing. They're strong women, especially Serena. I don't think he was trying to be racist; I think he was trying to be funny. That's the easiest tag to throw on people: "You're a racist." It's hard for me because I've known people who were labeled that way who clearly are not. Not the least of which is Kerry

Collins. When he came to the Giants, that's all anybody said, "You got to watch out for him. He's a bad guy. He's a racist." I went in with an open mind about Kerry, not prejudging him. To this day, Kerry and I are very close—and he's the furthest thing from a racist.

Sid cracks me up all the time. He's real. He's not faking his enthusiasm for something. That's how he really is. Coming from Virginia, everything was shocking when I first came to New York. Listening to talk radio and getting to know him was shocking, because everything was in fast-forward. I was like, "Can we slow down a minute? Can we take a breath? I didn't hear what you said three minutes ago and you're still talking." We're polar opposites. You wouldn't think we'd be as friendly and close as we are. He's a white guy from Brooklyn who talks a mile a minute and is super opinionated. We don't have a lot in common. I'm an African American from the South on the other side of his profession. But we hit it off mainly because we're real with each other. He was never afraid to question, in a legitimate way, not in a malicious way, when things were going badly with me. When I was having my fumbling problems, he was always straightforward with me. He wanted to hear my reasoning before opining on it. I always appreciated that, because one thing I always said was, "Don't make excuses for me. Just ask me the question and I'll tell you the answer. I'm not running away from it." It's interesting because he's so different. But if you're just around the same people like yourself, you kind of get bored.

Why Philadelphia Fans
Are the Worst People
on the Face of the Earth

The Philadelphia Eagles, I hate those cocksuckers.

It was the year the Giants won the Super Bowl, 1990. We started that year 10–0. My father, Sal, Richie, and I decided to go to Philly to watch a game. We went there early because we found out that the Marriott Hotel across the street from the old Vet had a great brunch at 11:00 in the morning on Sundays. So we went there and had a really nice brunch at the hotel before heading into Veteran's Stadium. I made the mistake of wearing a Lawrence Taylor jersey—a bunch of us were wearing Giants stuff—and the Philly fans were the most vicious, vile, lowlife fans you ever saw. I mean, yelling curse words and spitting at us, guys drinking Jack Daniels with their egg sandwiches at 8:00 in the morning. Just fucking nasty, man.

They even tipped my car over. It was a little Toyota, and the maniacs tipped the fucking thing over. My car was upside down! They yelled at us and spit on us all game long. Honestly, at one point I feared for my life. It was that vile, that nasty, that disgusting. I vowed I would never go back to an Eagles game at the Vet. We were up in the 700 section at Veteran's Stadium in Philadelphia, and it was filled with the biggest lowlifes in the history of professional sports.

The Eagles beat the shit out of us that day. You'd think that them beating the shit out of us and Randall Cunningham going nuts, would be all they needed to stick in a New York Giants fan's face. We were undefeated, we were in first place, and they were kicking our ass. You think that would be enough. But it still wasn't enough for them. They were still throwing shit at us. It was unbelievable. I've been to a lot of sporting events in a lot of cities where I've rooted for the opposing team; it gets a little hairy sometimes, but what happened in Philadelphia was just above and beyond.

I don't like Dallas—obviously, the Giants and Cowboys have a nice little rivalry, but we have never played them in a playoff game outside of a few years ago. The Redskins are fine because we beat them a couple of times on the way to Super Bowls. Bill Parcells had his success against Joe Gibbs. To me, the one team I despise more than any other, the one city I despise, is Philadelphia. I hate every single one of their teams: the Flyers as a Rangers fan, the Phillies as a Mets fan. Okay, the Sixers don't matter, because I love Julius Erving.

But I *hated* the Eagles. I guess it goes all the way back to Chuck Bednarik knocking out Frank Gifford. I wasn't born until 20 years after that, but even now that bothers me. Even when we were good there wasn't a game where either Clyde Simmons or Reggie White or Jerome Brown, Seth Joyner at linebacker, and Andre Waters at safety didn't make Phil Simms fumble. Those Buddy Ryan teams were the teams I hated most. Let me put it in the proper perspective: I'd much rather take a walk in Fallujah, at 3:00 AM than go to a Philadelphia Eagles game in Philadelphia. I'd feel safer. How about that? I'd feel safer wearing a yarmulke at a bar mitzvah in Baghdad than wearing an L.T. jersey in Philadelphia.

By the way, the Eagles are another team that hasn't won shit. I know Donovan McNabb has gotten them to the Super Bowl and they've been to something like 30 NFC championship games. But how about winning one, you know? We've won three times since 1986. The Eagles haven't won dick. As much as I hate the Eagles and I hate the franchise and everything about them, I happen to like Donovan because I think he gets a raw deal. I don't think he gets the credit he deserves. But win something, man! Fucking win something!

I despise the Phillies, too, but the Eagles are on a totally different level of hatred. I don't hate the 76ers. In fact, the Sixers team with Moses Malone, Andrew Toney, Maurice Cheeks, Julius Erving, Marc Iavaroni, and Bobby Jones, coached by Billy Cunningham, was among my favorite teams of all time. The Knicks and Sixers have never been good at the same time, so that's helped. And Julius Erving is one of my all-time favorite players, so I don't have that hatred of the Sixers. The Phillies, on the other hand, I can't stand, although I'm not going to lie. I was happy for Tug McGraw when he won a World Series with them in 1980. Look, the Braves were the team that have for the most part won the division every single year in the last 15 years, and the Mets-Braves have really been the more significant rivalry over the last 15 years or so, but definitely I hate the Phillies. I also hate them because of the trade the Mets made back in 1990, sending Lenny Dykstra and Roger McDowell for that bum Juan Samuel, one of the worst trades in Mets history.

Shaquille O'Neal is a guy I've never rooted for. He's a big, fat, lazy loudmouth, and what he did to the city of Miami is disgusting. He was a nice player in Orlando and Los Angeles, and I never had a rooting interest in him one way or the other. But when he came to Miami and promised to deliver a championship and then won a championship in 2006 by just hopping on Dwyane Wade's back—because Dwyane Wade single-handedly won that championship—that just disgusted me. If you look back at Shaq's numbers in that series against Dallas they were embarrassing—and he was getting more than $20 million a year! Shaq wanted to take some of the credit for winning the championship—after all, he promised!—

then he stank the next couple of seasons, not even showing up half the time. He readily admitted that he didn't care about the regular season, that he wanted to get himself in shape for the playoffs. But of course, by the time the playoffs came along, he was so out of shape from not trying during the regular season he couldn't do a goddamn thing anyway. And then after a while the Heat stopped making the playoffs altogether. Then he went to Phoenix because the Heat thought, *He's washed up, he's finished, at least we won a championship*, and he goes to the All-Star Game (deservedly so, by the way). Now it's obvious to Heat fans that for about a two-year period in Miami, he didn't want to play, Pat Riley couldn't stand him and couldn't wait to get rid of him. Shaq has never left a place where he didn't have something nasty to say on the way out. I can't stand guys like that.

And of course, there's T.O. I can't think of an athlete I like less than Terrell Owens. He's my least favorite player, maybe ever. He's another jerk-off. Some people say there's something brilliant about the way he sells himself. There's *nothing* brilliant about the guy. Mike Tyson, to me, was somewhat brilliant. Because when Mike Tyson went up there and said, "I'm going to eat your children" before the Lennox Lewis fight, you knew it was calculated. He knew that in some way he had to get that thing going so they could promote that fight, and it turned out to be a monster success, both live in Memphis and on television. Of course, I have no proof of this, but I believe Mike Tyson, for as crazy as he is—and he's a madman—had a lot of that stuff figured. He said a lot of that shit just to make people angry. And that's fine. But when T.O. goes out there and blasts his own quarterback, what is good about that? When T.O. goes out and blasts Jeff Garcia or Donovan McNabb or Tony Romo, how does that help? What is smart about that? What is refreshing about that? Listen, I don't care if you blast other teams or if you have a big mouth. That's fine. But don't blast your own players. You just don't do that. That's where I draw the line with T.O., and he's done it everywhere he's been. I don't mind trash talkers, but don't trash your own teammates.

Another guy I can't stand is Barry Bonds. Actually, I think he's among my least-favorite athletes ever. Not because he took steroids, but because I've heard countless stories of him refusing to sign autographs and because of the way he treats the media. I dealt with Barry once at an All-Star Game, and he shunned me, as well. He's just not a good guy. I understand he was a baby, and his father Bobby and godfather Willie Mays taught him to be that way. They told him, "Watch out. People are out to get you" so that didn't happen by accident. But nobody likes that guy. *Nobody*. I can never root for that guy. It has nothing at all to do with the steroids. He's just a total jerk-off.

Shylocks, Stu Feiner's Monkey, and the Absolute Lunacy of Sports Betting

I started betting when I was 11 years old, when I made my first teaser bet. And I remember the first bet that killed me. It wasn't for a lot of money. It was a several years later, and Georgetown was playing North Carolina in college basketball—that championship game when fucking Freddie Brown threw the pass right to James Worthy. That one hit me hard. Freddie Brown threw the pass to a wide-open James Worthy. And why was he wide open? Because he played for the other team! That was the game in which Michael Jordan, Sam Perkins, Jimmy Black, James Worthy, and all those guys beat Patrick Ewing and Sleepy Floyd and Georgetown. I was a Big East fan growing up—St. John's and Chris Mullin—so I watched a lot of Georgetown games. I figured, *Ewing and Floyd, these guys are not going to lose*. And then Freddie Brown throws the pass right to James Worthy. That's the first one I remember that hurt. I was in high school, and I bet a couple of thousand dollars with my buddy Yitzy (his name was Isaac, but we called him Yitzy) at Solomon Schechter.

My buddies at Poly Prep were into gambling already. It just seemed exciting at the time, and it was. In Brooklyn in the late 1970s and early 1980s, it was not tough to find a bookie on any corner. I went to school in Bay Ridge so it was easy to gamble, and I liked it. The juices got flowing.

I had some really good paydays, but I lost most of the time. It cost me a lot of grief, personally and professionally, over the years. It's a horrible thing, actually. It's fun every now and then—you win a couple of games and it certainly adds more excitement to sports—but truth be told, it's a horrible, horrible addiction. It's beaten me up over the years. I have friends who have lost wives and lost kids and lost hope and lost jobs. It's not a funny thing. You have fun with it when you start out, but when you start betting every single day on every single game, then it starts getting a little fucking out of hand.

I had the Broncos when they lost 55–10 to the Niners in the Super Bowl. That was over early. One of the largest bets I ever won, believe it or not, was the Giants playing the Niners in 1991. The Giants had just beaten Buffalo in the Super Bowl. Bill Parcells left, and Ray Handley took over, announcing that Jeff Hostetler would be the starting quarterback. In his first game the Giants played the Niners on *Monday Night Football*. The Giants won 16–14 and I laid a point and a half. I went to that game with my dad. They had just won the Super Bowl, it's a home game, and they won on a field goal. They beat 'em by two on a late fucking field goal, and that was one of the biggest paydays I ever had—for one game at least.

I've bet on thousands and thousands of games. It's been an ongoing problem my whole life. I bet on everything—baseball, basketball, hockey, and football, anything. I remember a baseball game in 2006. The Padres were playing the Dodgers, and Trevor Hoffman was pitching for San Diego. The Padres were leading 9–5, and the Dodgers hit four straight home runs in the bottom of the ninth to tie it. Nomar Garciaparra hit one in the tenth and the Dodgers won the game 11–10. I had the Padres.

The Steelers-Cowboys Super Bowl in which officials called offensive pass interference on Michael Irvin when he caught a touchdown pass in the end zone, and they called it back—that one fucking hurt me. That was the Neil O'Donnell game. He kept finding a wide-open Larry Brown, who played for the other team.

The most I bet on one game was $10,000. I did that a couple of times. Once was on the Pittsburgh-Seattle Super Bowl. I took Pittsburgh, and I won that one, 10 grand. That game got very, very close, and to be honest I got lucky because Seattle got jobbed by the referees a number of times. There were some bad calls in that game. But I could absolutely care less.

Over the years, I lost money to bookmakers and borrowed money from shylocks. I lost big dollars to bookmakers and went out on the street. If I couldn't borrow the money from friends or family, I would go to shylocks and pay those fucking ridiculous percentages. When you don't pay the bank on time, the worst thing that's going to happen is that you get a phone call at your house. When you have a certain date you're supposed to meet a shylock with a certain amount of money? Well, it's not like the old *Goodfellas* days. It's not the Wild West. They don't just fucking kill you, but they're certainly not as patient or as nice about it as the bank.

I've been uncomfortable. I've had guys call my house, even when I was married, or meet me outside of work, that type of thing. That happened a bunch of times over the years. But I never really borrowed enough or lost enough to risk bodily harm. But in my lifetime, I've lost in the hundreds of thousands of dollars; there's no question about it.

I think addicts, whatever it is they like doing, are always going to say you never miss the bad times or the repercussions. I've been to rehab, and people say, "I don't miss coke. I don't miss this and that." I think they do miss coke. I think, at the end of the day, you do miss what gave you all the trouble in the first place. But what you never miss are the repercussions and the horrendous damage you do to yourself and anybody who cares about you.

You get to the point where you can taste that in your mouth. Even if you do occasionally watch games and think to yourself, *Damn, I would have had that one*, if you've done enough damage you may you get to the point where it's just not worth the risk.

Whatever the addiction is, anybody who tells you, "I don't miss that at all. I hate it," is lying, I think. Every addict, at least once in a while, misses his addiction. The key is realizing that it's going to destroy them and to remember the damage more clearly than the win they might have had 10 years ago.

It's tough during football season. I don't care where you are or what show you're on. You're pretty much obligated to bring on a handicapper every Friday, which I've done—because that's what people want to hear. Being in the business where people are calling, breaking down games, and analyzing them. Me talking to people about that makes it more difficult. Even if the discussion is not about gambling *per se*, it's still out there.

You hear announcers all the time. Al Michaels is guilty of that. Brent Musburger, every single time, will start off a broadcast that way ("Here in Piscataway, New Jersey, today Rutgers takes on Seton Hall. Rutgers is nearly a double-digit favorite.") I think that because of our proximity to all that information, a lot of guys who are sports hosts gamble.

I'm in the locker room, I know these guys, and I know what's going on. There have been instances when I knew guys have been nicked up, times when they haven't even disclosed to the press just how nicked up they were, and I've acted on it. I've been privy to some of that information over the last 10 to 12 years. Let me tell you where it gets you: nowhere. It doesn't mean shit. You know José Canseco says 80 percent of baseball is on steroids. That's probably a gross exaggeration. I would say 70 percent of sports hosts gamble on some sport at some point, maybe 80 percent. None of them win, because at the end of the day having too much information becomes a detriment.

I'll never forget when they did that thing on HBO's *Real Sports* with Stu Feiner. You call his service out of Long Island, and he gives you his picks. He was making picks against a monkey—an actual monkey—and the monkey beat him! Stu's on the show with all the information he gathered. He says, "I'm talking to this guy and that guy, and buy my picks. I've got my four-star pick of the week, the five-star pick of the week. I'll make you $10,000," and on and on—and he lost to the monkey. Sometimes knowing too much is detrimental. The guys with the girlfriends know what I'm talking about. The girls say, "I kind of like the colors of those uniforms," and the guys say, "But that team stinks." And the girlfriend's team wins.

I always felt like because I was in the business I had the edge on the average guy calling up from his living room on Sunday because I spoke to the coaches this week, or I spoke to the players this week. And truth be told, it doesn't matter. The guy's girlfriend could pick the games, or the guy's eight-year-old son. It doesn't matter.

I don't go on the radio and make it sound like I know everything. First of all, 99 percent of my listeners know me. My career's been a pretty open book. You go on Wikipedia right now and look up my name and it talks about the triple addiction of gambling, cocaine, and drinking. I've talked about it on the air, on my own shows, on *Imus*. It's out there. When people call, I make it very clear, "Hey listen, I haven't exactly fared well over the years. I know what's going on, I know every player, I'm as well-versed as anyone in the country, if not more, but that doesn't really mean I can tell you who's going to win. Now, with that said, I would lay the six and a half." I'm always going to give them the opinion, but I always start with a disclaimer. Just because I just spoke to [Packers coach] Mike McCarthy doesn't mean I know any more than you do. With that said, lay the points. I'll come on and say, "Listen, I'm a guy who's down probably $3 million during my career so I don't know why you want my pick, but with that said, you've got to bet everything you got, bet the house, bet the ranch, bet the kids, bet the mortgage the Packers are going to win by three touchdowns."

I can't stand reformists. I can't stand it. I don't like people who smoked for 40 years, and then all of a sudden they're in a restaurant, somebody's smoking behind them, and they want him kicked out.

I don't preach to anybody. For me to preach about that stuff would be pretty hypocritical. Do I tell people every now and then about the dangers? Do they know what's happened to me? Absolutely. I've had people call me on the air about a Packers-Bengals game. That's one thing. But I've had people contact me off the air, send me e-mails and say, "Hey listen, Sid, I know you used to have troubles here and there but you're still serving as an inspiration because you're out there, talking about these things and I struggle every single day." I still don't preach, but I talk about it more realistically about what it can do to you and what I've done to try to combat it. I've had lots of responses to that. I've had lots of e-mails from people talking about drinking and drugging and gambling. On the air, it's a big joke. Off the air and in that situation I certainly try to tell them what I've been through and what could be in store for them if they don't get help.

I've gone back and forth to Gamblers Anonymous a bunch of times. Started back in 1992 in Sheepshead Bay in Brooklyn. I went back to it in 1997 in Boca, and I go now too. Three times now I've left and come back to the program. I'm not embarrassed to say it's part of my life now.

Is It Better to Have Bet and Lost Than Never to Have Bet at All?

People are often impressed with my sports knowledge. Believe it or not, even though my career kind of goes down the middle, the controversial Sid Rosenberg, there are still lots of fans, FAN fans, Miami fans, outside the *Imus* stuff, who would constantly praise me for sports knowledge. They would say, "How do you know all that?"

I don't need to bet on the Mets to watch them; I don't need to bet on the Giants to watch them, the Rangers or the Knicks. Even though I'm a sports enthusiast and I love my teams, if I was going to be totally honest I would say the reason why I got to know so much about sports is because I gambled at an early age.

I was up late watching the Dodgers and the Padres as a teenager because when you have money on the game, you have a rooting interest. While most kids in New York didn't know who the fuck played in those lineups, I was up at 11:30 at night watching those games, and I'm very aware of who's on those teams. It didn't matter what sport it was. I laid goals in hockey, I laid points in basketball, runs in baseball, points in football—I bet it all. I was an enthusiast of teams in every single sport, but what really made me a student of the games was the money I had on them.

It's no different than guys with fantasy football nowadays. All of a sudden, every football geek can tell you the third receiver on the Atlanta Falcons because of fantasy—which is gambling, by the way. Anybody who tells you it's not is being naïve. It's gambling. You're gambling on individual performances, but at the end of the day it's no different than betting on the outcome of a game.

You can say what you want, but the NFL knows it. The NFL makes me laugh. They suspend people, like Alex Karras and Paul Hornung, to take it way back, but they don't want anything to do with the betting aspect of the game. I saw Stephen A. Smith a while back on television, and he had this guy on, Brandon Lang, who is a tout, a handicapper. Who is Brandon Lang? In the movie with Matthew McConaughey and Al Pacino, *Two for the Money*, McConaughey plays a pretty good college quarterback on the way to big money in the pros who rips up his knee and has to retire from the game. He ends up picking games here and there. He knows the sport, he played the sport, and he does very, very well. Pacino is a big-time odds guy up in New York who becomes aware of this guy and hires him to come to New York. These guys make millions and millions until he stops picking well. And then he loses it all and nearly gets killed. McConaughey's character was based on the real life of Brandon Lang.

Lang was a guest on the now-defunct *Quite Frankly with Stephen A. Smith* show, and he made the point that the reason any sport is popular is because of gambling. Stephen A. Smith was appalled, saying, "That's ridiculous. I've never bet on anything in my whole life, and I'm on ESPN. I'm in sports." I remember sitting there and saying, "What a jerk-off." First of all, I think Stephen A. Smith is a jerk-off anyway. A loudmouth, fucking jerk-off. But what a moron. I mean, c'mon, don't be stupid! Lang was absolutely right: the reason why sports are so popular today is because of gambling. Now obviously there's more gambling in the NFL. But if you look at the casinos out in Las Vegas, plenty of bets are laid on baseball every single day. Not to mention the burgeoning fantasy baseball stuff. I can't tell you people are betting a lot on hockey, but with Internet gambling, people are gambling all over the world.

People in England bet on tennis and soccer and the fucking stock market.

I'll fight people to the death over this. For every person who hasn't gambled, I'll find you 50 guys who have either played fantasy sports or dabbled in gambling. People gamble, period. I believe it's like prostitution and drugs. Prostitution, marijuana, and gambling should be legalized in every state today. Because everybody does it—everybody—and there's plenty of money in it. Why not make money on it instead of having that revenue go offshore to people in fucking Costa Rica and other countries?

Until my dying day, I will maintain that gambling is what drives sports. Why would anybody buy the Direct TV NFL Sunday Ticket? Why would a Giants fan buy it? Because he loves football? Because he's glued to the set when the Chargers are playing the Raiders at 4:30 that afternoon? No. Because he gambled on the game or because he's got Antonio Gates at tight end on his fantasy team. Why, if you're a Mets fan, would you watch the Giants and Dodgers at 11:30 PM? Unless of course you're Chris Russo and you're a Giants fan. The NBA League Pass, the NHL Center Ice—all those things are geared towards the gamblers. I maintain that if everybody was worried only about his own team, or if they had a lukewarm interest in their sport, they wouldn't be shelling out serious money every single month to buy all these fucking TV packages.

If You Think the Other Guy
Looks Bad, You Should See Me

Bernard McGuirk is the producer of the *Imus* show. He and I would always go back and forth with each other—that was kind of our role on the show. Stuff like "You Jew"/"You Mick." From day one and to today, Bernie and I absolutely love each other. We would say outrageous things on the air, and we always went back and forth with each other all the time—and Imus loved it. He loved the tension between Bernie and me on the air. It would get nasty once in a while, but it was always for the show.

Danielle and I were living in Chelsea at the time, on Eighth Avenue between 20th and 21st Streets. I became a member of the Chelsea Piers gym, and I was working out pretty hard. Bernie is in great shape. He does like marathons and triathlons and all that type of shit. He's a maniac. Basically it started on the air as "Fuck you, I'll kick your ass," and this whole fight thing got rolling. We decided, let's do it in the ring. That's something Howard Stern did before us with Stuttering John and Cabbie years and years beforehand. Not that we copied Howard, mind you, but this was sort of in the same vein. Now there are two *Imus* guys going back and forth with each other.

Bob Gelb, who was a salesman and a former producer of *Mike and the Mad Dog* for many years, came up with *The Fear at the*

Pier, set for October 3, 2003. They had camera crews from MSNBC follow Bernie down to his gym while he was working out. They had camera crews from MSNBC follow me down to Chelsea Piers to film me while I was working out. There was a lot of trash talking on the *Imus* show for months leading up to this fight. As it turned out, Imus ended up selling the tickets for $500 apiece. They had 500 seats, and all the money was going to the Imus Ranch—every single dime was going to charity. We sold out all 500 seats, so we literally raised a quarter of a million dollars that day. It was worth getting my fucking ass kicked to raise a quarter of a million dollars for kids with cancer.

We just were at each other's throats for two, three months at a time, the bits and the back and forth. When we announced we were going to do this fight in the early summer of 2003. In July 2003 I moved from Manhattan to Tenafly, New Jersey, so I wasn't really going to Chelsea Piers to work out anymore. At the same time, my wife became pregnant with our first child, Ava. So I had moved to New Jersey, Danielle was pregnant, and a month before the fight I'm miles and miles away from the gym I belong to, at home with my pregnant wife eating ice cream and Chinese food at midnight. All this bravado from when I was in good shape and strong and lifting good weight, and it turned to shit right before the fight. Bernie, on the other hand, worked out like a maniac the whole time.

Growing up, I got into a million fights because I was always drunk and high and out of control. I remember one time at the Palladium, I got hit over the head with a Heineken bottle and fell down all the stairs. I went out to a different club in the city every Friday night, and I came home every Saturday morning bleeding and beat up. I had a habit of starting fights. I had a habit of getting drunk and out of control—and if I didn't instigate the fight, I certainly didn't stop it, and then I would expect my friends to do the damage. I was one of those guys, "Fuck you, fuck you" who always had nine guys behind him. But I was always getting my ass kicked as a kid. They used to dance on the top of speakers at nightclubs in Manhattan when I was growing up, so I'd come home and tell my father, "I fell off the speaker." There would be glass in my forehead, stuff like that. It was awful. I'm from Brooklyn, and I always thought I was a tough guy even though I don't think I've ever won a fight in my whole life.

When I was 10 years old, I hit a kid in the face with a Wiffle ball bat because he was messing with me and my friend Craig Siedman. We went to Woodlands, a bungalow colony in upstate New York, every summer. We were playing with these kids, and this kid kept picking on us. I told him, "You keep it up, I'm going to hit you in the face with this bat." And I did it! His name was Mitchell. To this day the guy is still half blind out of his right eye because I smacked him the face with that Wiffle ball bat. I went to camp with him, and he was a pain in the ass and a bully. He needed a bunch of stitches and was in the hospital and lost vision in that eye. I saw him 10 years later. He still couldn't see that well.

I was in fights all the time, but I never won anything. With Bernie, I figured it would be good for the show. How much would Bernie really beat me up, you know? I was taking Creatine—I was taking all sort of enhancers. I really thought I was going to be able to beat him.

That morning I woke up very nervous. I got to the ring at like 5:45 AM. All the seats were set up and the ring was set up and I thought, *Holy shit*. It was surreal, like *What the fuck am I doing? I'm going to be on MSNBC all over the world getting my fucking face punched in? Am I nuts?*

It was supposed to be a three-round fight, but by the middle of the third round they called it. I had a broken nose and a concussion. I was pretty fucked up and bleeding pretty good. I'll never forget—it was the middle of the third round, and Lee Davis, he was the general manager of WFAN at the time, I saw him jumping up and down throwing his hands up in the air yelling, "Stop the fight!" because he probably felt I was going to sue CBS. I think he was literally nervous he was going to have a problem on his hands if I got too fucked up. I hadn't taken out any insurance. We did sign something for the actual boxing commission. Lee Davis wanted to stop the fight in the second round. I said, "No, you're not stopping this fight." I finished the second round, came out for the third round, and got pummeled again.

I've broken my nose a few times. I had been hit by a baseball but never by somebody who hit me with a straight right to the face. He literally punched my face and broke my nose. It hurt. I got the concussion midway through the second round, probably. I took a lot of shots to the head. I remember being really fuzzy and cloudy with a headache. Even after, driving home to New Jersey by myself, I stopped at the diner to get some pancakes that morning. Reading the menu was blurry to me. When I couldn't even read the menu, that's when I said to myself, *Holy shit, there must be some neurological damage here.*

Imus loved it. It was a huge day for his show, he raised a lot of money for his ranch, and he was really happy, thanking me for putting my life on the line. I said, "I don't feel too good, I-man. I think I might take tomorrow off." He was like, "No, we definitely want you there tomorrow. We want you there all fucked up. If you're woozy and fucked up, even better." I got up at like 4:45 the next morning and went to work. I felt like shit, I still had a headache, and I still felt kind of woozy. I was black and blue and beat up, but I was on the air the next morning.

There are worse guys to get beat up by than Bernie. First of all, I think Bernie is brilliant. With a lot of the stuff that goes on during the *Imus* show, the one guy who seems to be up on everything is Bernie. There's really nothing you can't discuss with him. He'll know something about anything that's going on. On the political stuff he's great, the news stuff he's great—even the sports stuff. He's the one guy on that show, more than Imus or Charles McCord or anybody, who knows what's going on. Bernie helps prepare Imus and is just a smart guy. He's wickedly funny, he's not afraid to be controversial, he's not afraid to stick his head out there, and much like me, a lot of times Bernie will say things that maybe the audience is thinking and maybe even Imus is thinking, but he's crazy enough to say it.

Some of my best moments on the *Imus* show were with Bernie, because he knew how to play me and how to get me going. You would think he might look at me like, "Here's another young gun who's kind of controversial and not afraid to say shit. This guy's stealing some of my thunder," and he was never like that. There was never a threat or jealousy of any kind.

He's every bit as good as anybody else on that show when it comes to doing a prepared bit, but in terms of being spontaneous, I think Bernie's as funny as anybody in the business. Look, a lot of times it's easy for Artie Lange to be funny on the *Howard Stern Show* because they're talking about comedians or actresses or actors, things that are funny. Bernie's able to take something that's political in nature that's not inherently funny and make it funny.

WE NOW INTERRUPT OUR REGULARLY SCHEDULED BROADCAST FOR A WORD FROM…

BERNARD McGUIRK, Producer, *Imus in the Morning*

It was 2001. Mark Chernoff brought Sid in. He had been on some unlistenable morning sports talk show on WNEW called *Sports Guys*. One of the guys he was with was Craig Carton. It was just one of those awful, horrible shows. It was like, "You hate the Giants? Call us!" Some guy calls in and goes, "Giants suck!" and they go, "Yeah, that's right, we're the Sports Guys!" It was a bunch of muttonheads ranting and raving about nothing. But in any case, it was a good springboard for a couple of guys. Craig has been pretty successful over there at FAN, much to the chagrin of Sid, I would imagine. Sid was introduced to us, did a couple of fill-in shows when Warner

Wolf was out, and immediately we recognized the guy's a natural. He's way off the hook—a great talker, fast talker. He's got that Jewish Brooklyn accent and is just a fast-talking knucklehead. We liked him immediately. We knew he had wacky potential, and he certainly didn't disappoint.

We started to use Sid. We cut back on Warner, actually. We had them alternate until we got to the point we decided we'd like to have Sid full time. That happened to coincide with an offer Warner got at Channel 2—at Mr. Imus' prodding. Imus was tight with a couple of WCBS executives, they offered Warner a job back on TV, and it all worked out. Warner went back to TV, and Sid became the full-time sportscaster on the *Imus in the Morning* program. He was amazing. He had boundless energy. We now know it had a lot to do with illicit substances, including those stupid diet pills that were popular a few years ago, TrimSpa. That had a lot to do with his amazing energy. He'd eat 'em like M&Ms. I did them occasionally; it was definitely like doing bust-out speed. It was touted as being healthy, but it had Ephedra in it. You could catch a stroke from too much of that crap. He was chewing gum and his eyes were darting around, but it worked. On air he came up big. He was good, he was funny, he was feisty, and he was contentious. He and I used to go at it back and forth, the Jew versus the Gentile, the Jew versus the goy. We had some pretty good on-air battles, but we were friends throughout. It was all for show. We thought we knew what made for a good listen—and that was conflict—and we provided it. We created the impression that we hated each other and that's what led up to the time when we fought each other in the boxing ring.

There was a certain amount of machismo on both our parts because we were talking it up on the air. I played basketball with him on WFAN's basketball team with Ed Coleman and those guys, and Sid demonstrated himself to be a very good athlete. He was hitting three-pointers; he was a very good basketball player. So I thought he had some athletic skills. I took it seriously, and he guaranteed that he was going to knock me out in the first round, he was going to break my nose, so damn right I took it very seriously! I trained with Randy Gordon of the New York State Boxing Commission. He used to train Larry Holmes. I knew Sid was taking steroids, the knucklehead, and he was a good athlete—so I took it very seriously.

One of the highlights was during the weigh-in, on the air, when I presented him with an autographed athletic cup for his wife. I think he got angry, and it sort of motivated him a little to beat my ass. He tried to save face. I think he thought he could beat me. He was pretty surprised when he started taking punches and they hurt. I beat him to a pulp. It was easy. I would throw feints and he would fall for them, and then I'd "boom" hit him with the other hand. Or I'd fake I was going to punch him in his nose. He'd raise his hands, and I'd smack him in the stomach. He'd drop his hands, and I'd punch him in the face again. I kind of felt bad, but I wasn't going to slow down until someone threw the towel in. But he was game, he didn't give up. He was looking for that one knockout blow. It didn't come. The only blow he got was on the street corner later that night, perhaps.

It ended up with management forcing it to a stop after about two and a half rounds because they were worried they were going to get sued if he died. I would have had to knock him unconscious, because he wasn't going to give up. I think he won people over just by that display of courage. He had the heart of a lion.

Chris Russo hated him because he saw him as a threat on the air, legitimately. Sid is a great talent. It's terrible how he self-destructed. It could have been him in the morning right now or in the afternoon or anywhere. It's just awful, sad. He's on his way back, but he would have been in New York right now. From what I understand, Mike Francesa runs hot and cold, but he knows talent when he sees it. They didn't always get along back at WFAN, Francesa and Sid, but given the opportunity to have a guy like that on your team, Francesa's no fool. He covers sports, he knows something about winning and losing and that's why he was more than open to the idea of having Sid cohost his show because the guy's an incredible talent. He's a natural. I haven't seen many guys like that in this business, and I've been in it for more than 20 years now.

Sid, in my humble opinion, is too close to what Russo is. The two of them are almost cut from the same cloth, except Sid is a street-smart version of Russo. Russo's on the up-and-up, he's cornier, but they're both fast-talking sports guys, and the way they talk is funny. Sid is willing to get down in the gutter with you and mix it up, whereas Russo will take a pass. Sid's a coke-snorting whack-job. At least he was.

We've had him on with Imus. He's welcome to call in. He's a funny guy. It's all about redemption. Even Michael Vick gets a second chance. That's what makes this country great. When he was fired, he was in that car with his family, with a "For Sale" sign on his house. He had declared bankruptcy, he's heading south, and it doesn't get any more rock bottom than that. He headed down to live with the in-laws in Florida—no job, no nothing. He paid a price, is still paying it in a way. Everybody deserves a second chance, especially a guy like that, who's kept his nose clean in Miami, one of the most drug-addled cities in the country. He's been a good boy. So yeah, we put him on. We on the *Imus in the Morning* program got a second chance, and he deserves a second chance. Imus likes him a lot, plus it's a quid pro quo—when he comes on he's good. We put a place at the table for him, and then he brings something to the table. He's not a charity case. He's actually funny. It's just the way he talks, that fast-talking Brooklyn accent. You and I can say something, but the way he says it makes it funny. He is like an animated character. It's an intangible I can't really articulate very well that he has, but he's got it. If Damon Runyon were alive today and creating characters, Sid Rosenberg would be one of them.

Back then I thought we were sort of, not invincible, but there was nobody out there, nobody saying, "Don't do this, don't do that." You have to remember, it was during the era of Howard Stern and *Opie and Anthony*. We were competing with those types of shows, and for a long time nobody came down on anybody, the FCC, nobody. It was just a free-for-all, no holds barred. Amazingly, we were on MSNBC, a legitimate cable news operation, and yet nobody ever said anything. They let us do what we wanted. Nobody ever told us where the line was. The line was shifting, and I don't think we realized it.

When Sid said the line about the Williams sisters I guess it sounded rough, but it just didn't seem to me like a fireable type of offense. It was definitely out there and a big "Whoa." But nobody called for his firing. There were a couple of reports in the paper, and Imus made him apologize and write a letter and read it on air. It was no corporate thing. There was no outcry from any civil rights groups or anything like that. It wasn't until the Kylie Minogue comment that he got fired.

I thought he was funny. He was close to the line. Just a natural talent, conversant in entertainment, sports, and politics, and I didn't think he would stray over the line. I wasn't worried about him. In retrospect, I probably should have been.

It would be a natural reaction for me to have resented him, but the way I looked at it was that he was an asset, somebody I could play off of and play with, and that's exactly what it turned into. To my credit, I could have looked at him as a threat and thought, "They're going to shut me up and let this guy talk," but he opened up the discussion. He would introduce topics that otherwise would not have been introduced. He made everything funny. I could take the opposite point of view with whatever he took, and he could do the same with me. We realized it gave us the opportunity to go back and forth about a lot of the pop culture things and sports things Imus wouldn't be aware of or wouldn't have an opinion but I would. I never looked at him as a hostile or as some sort of invader or somebody I had to look over my shoulder and be worried about. I don't want to say anything negative about Imus; Sid just opened everything up. He would just introduce it, we would run with it, and it was hilarious. Usually it would degenerate into an ethnic thing or something stupid like that. Or I was hosing his wife or he was hosing his wife. We tried to make it funny.

Absolutely, I miss him. I'd love to have him back full time. Obviously I love Warner Wolf, but it's a different kind of humor. I absolutely miss Sid. I'd love to do a show with him. I think we could do a great show together, the two of us. I think he elevates me. He's an entertainer, and he knows what's funny. He would do it for the good of the show, and that's why sometimes he'd get himself in trouble. He's not a racist or a misogynist. In his juvenile way he would just go too far thinking he was funny, but a lot of people didn't think it was funny. He's not a hater at all; he's just a knucklehead who doesn't think sometimes before he opens his mouth.

I'd like to see him back in New York one day and back on the national stage, because he's just a natural. In New York you have a very conservative organization like Disney and then one or two people over at CBS. There aren't any other outlets really in the city. But things will change. I predict he'll be back. I'm sure he will be.

How I Met the One Woman in the World Who Can Put Up with Me

I don't think women like me. This could trace back to my Venus and Serena Williams comment in 2001, though that was more of a racial thing—if you ask the press at least. Still, Venus and Serena *are* both women. I made that Kylie Minogue comment back in 2005. She's a woman. Unfortunately, some of the comments I have made—which had nothing to do with gender—were aimed at women. When you combine them with my propensity to debate things like, "She's bangable/she's not bangable, she's hot/she's not hot"—well, let's just say the National Organization for Women is not asking me to speak at any of their events anytime soon, and leave it at that.

It really aggravates me, but I can see to a certain extent why a woman would think that I am sexist. I don't think I'm as bad as some of the media outlets make me out to be. My wife Danielle gets aggravated once in a while. She is a very strong woman. She's not a member of NOW or anything like that, but she believes women deserve more credit and should be treated better in the media—and she's pretty boisterous about that at home. She has been pissed off at me in the past, yes. Even though she knows it's part of the shtick, there have been times when I'll come home or I'll get a call and she'll say, "Really nice, what you said about that lady," or "You have a daughter, and you're talking like that?" Sure,

I've gotten that call. And I'd remind her that Howard Stern got away with that stuff all the time. And she'd remind me, "Guess what, Howard Stern is divorced and he's worth $500 million." That would be the end of that. I'm not divorced yet (although she could make that happen) and I'm not worth nearly that type of money. That was always my fallback, "But Howard..." and she'd say, "You're not Howard. Not even close."

There's a misconception that all I wanted to talk about was hot broads and that I flirted with the female callers. I mean, the only female caller I really remember is Doris from Rego Park, God rest her soul. She was an old lady who died of throat cancer. Look, on the *Imus* show, would I joke around with Bernadette Castro? Absolutely. Would I joke around with a Doris Kearns Goodwin? Absolutely. Did I make some jokes or sexual innuendo along the way? If you told me I did I'd say "probably," but it wasn't like it was a common occurrence.

So when people label me a chauvinist and a misogynist, what can I say? Sure, I said things on the air like, "This girl, I'd like to bang her," "This girl, I wouldn't bang her with your dick." If that makes me a misogynist, fine. Did I sometimes equate talent when it came to women with what they looked like physically? No doubt about it. But I was appealing to the guys my age at the time. Thirty- to 35-year-old guys like good-looking women. This is no mystery. And it wasn't like I was going out of my way to do it. If there was a *Sports Illustrated* story about the hot wives of NBA players I'd mention it. How could I not?

Danielle is an avid listener, and I talk about her on the air. I try not to get into too much stuff about our home life. There are two Sids. There's the Sid who's on the radio and the Sid who's at home who is decidedly not Radio Sid. People say to Danielle, "Wow, living with Sid's got to be nuts. That guy's crazy, he's funny, and he's maniacal. It's got to be crazy." And she sets them straight: "No. You have to understand, when Sid gets home, he's not like that at all. He's quiet, he's introspective, he watches TV, and that's it. The Sid you hear on the radio, that crazy man? That's not Sid."

I've often been asked the same thing. Those things you say on the air, do you really feel that way, or is that just Sid the character? I always say it's somewhere in the middle. When I get home I've got two kids and I've got my wife. Despite all of the craziness—the firings, the suspensions, the problems, and the controversies—we have a pretty normal family life. I have two children, and we have dinner together. I take my kids to camp and school. You might think that Radio Sid might never have any normalcy at home, with the drugs and the drinking and the gambling and the problems. All that has affected my family life, there's no doubt. It's made for problems. But for the most part, things are pretty vanilla.

Danielle likes her privacy. There have been times when Imus wanted her to come on the show, and she's always said no fucking way. She doesn't like that. She doesn't love the fact I even mention her name on the air or the fact she's an attorney. I know it sounds crazy because she's married to me, but she's a very moral person. She always does the right thing. I know there are a lot of attorneys out there that people think are crooked or depraved, but the fact is that she passed the bar and she has a moral obligation to the bar and to her profession. So for me to involve her in my craziness would be unfair, and she wants no part of it. So I just don't do it.

I told her a million times, "Don't listen, don't listen." She can tell me how great I am for 29 consecutive days, and then that one day when she's mad at me or not talking to me or telling me I'm a fucking asshole for saying something, I get furious. I want to scream, "Hey, you're an attorney, I don't walk into your courtroom and tell you how to defend your client, so don't fucking tell me what to say on the air."

* * *

I met Danielle when we were both at Kingsborough Community College. I hung out at a place called Captain Walters in Sheepshead

Bay on Emmons Avenue. It was the hot spot on Thursday nights. Pretty much everybody who lived in Brooklyn would go there. People even traveled from other boroughs. But it was predominantly a Brooklyn thing, especially if you were Jewish. Everybody knew everybody there.

So there was Danielle, the hottest girl in Brooklyn, and I was smitten. Of course, we'd never met. When we finally did, I was very outgoing with her. I was very popular, and I think she liked all that because the guy she had dated before me was very reserved and quiet. He could be in a bar for five hours, and you wouldn't have known he was there. I can't be in a bar for five minutes without everyone knowing I'm there. So she and I just kind of rolled the dice.

It was a very, very quick courtship. We had our engagement party in March 1992 and we married three months later. I was 25; Danielle was 23. We've been married close to 18 years. Usually, when people get married in their early twenties, it doesn't last. I don't have many friends in their forties who have been married for nearly 20 years like we are. The one over/under that Vegas would have won a lot of money on is this marriage, because everybody and their mother gave us "under a year." I mean, *everybody*. My own parents, my own family, her friends, her family—nobody thought it would last. We were so young and also volatile. Both of us are strongly opinionated, stubborn, and wild. Truth be told, as a gambling man—an unsuccessful one—I would have bet the house on the under. But we've made it work, and I'm a better man for it.

I hate to sound cliché because often people say, "Love is not enough." People love each other for years and years, but the divorce rate is nearly 60 percent. Obviously we must love each other, unless we're two crazy people.

I'm a guy who has had a lot of throwaway lines throughout my career. From my solo shows to my shows with partners to my *Imus* stuff, I have a million of them. But the one line that I guess wasn't a throwaway was when we said "For better or for worse." I don't think when you say it you really even think about it. You're standing up there just thinking, *Let's get the ring on, let's go on the honeymoon, and let's have a good time.* For what it's worth, for better or for worse has been the theme here for almost 18 years.

And I've put her though a lot. Danielle could have quit on this thing a long time ago, and nobody would have batted an eyelash. Nobody would have branded her a quitter. She's gone above and beyond. I put her through absolute hell. Thank God she stuck around. We have two beautiful children, and we've built a pretty good life. Obviously there have been ups and downs, maybe more than most people experience in three of four lifetimes, but I'm glad she stuck through it.

We were married in '92 and our daughter, Ava, was born in April 2004, nearly 12 years into our marriage. I was almost 37 years old. There were plenty of different reasons for that. Danielle, to her credit, has managed to mother two children and keep up a household and deal with all my bullshit and hold down a job, all at the same time. She went to law school in both New York and Florida and passed the bar on the first try in both states. That is virtually impossible. For my part, I've been to rehab twice since 1995 and didn't make good money in my profession until probably 2003, when I started my *Imus* thing and on into the middays with Jody McDonald. I had my issues, and she worked her ass off, burning the candle on three or four different ends, so it was unrealistic to have kids until much later.

Ava may not have changed me completely into an angel. I've gambled since then, I've drank since then, and I've done drugs since she was born. But it's been a lot less. I'm a much more responsible person now because of her. Although I'm far from perfect, and I could wake up any day and decide to do something crazy, that's just me. But I'm a much different person since Ava was born and even more since our son Gabriel was born on November 24, 2008.

I think I'm a great father. I'll never win Father of the Year, because it's difficult to do that if you're in rehab when your daughter is one year old. I've gambled money that could have gone to my kids. I've done drugs. I haven't been the perfect father, but I'm devoted to my kids. I spend a lot of time with them. I don't play golf because I think it's fucked up for a guy to disappear for six hours in a day. I'll go play basketball for an hour or two and by 10:00 AM I'm home with my wife and kids. I've had problems. I've gone out on weekend binges that have cost me jobs and people would think, *This guy's a fucking maniac.* They have no idea. Ninety-nine out of 100 days I'm home with my kids six, seven, eight hours a day. I take my daughter to school, I pick her up and help her with her work, and I take her to activities and birthday parties, to the park. My son is younger. I'm with him for hours and hours a day. I'm a great and doting father.

WE NOW INTERRUPT OUR REGULARLY SCHEDULED BROADCAST FOR A WORD FROM...

LESLEY VISSER, CBS Sports

I was an Imus devotee, and so I used to hear Sid. I would listen to him fairly regularly, and he always had something to say. Having worked at the *Boston Globe*, where everybody was really fast and quick and didn't spare your feelings, I was used to that kind of rapid repartee, or whatever the non-queer word for that is. I was used to people having an opinion and having a response, so I thought he was really interesting. Sid was funny. I had the same mixed reaction. I'm a Boston College, New England/Ohio, half WASP, half Catholic, so I did not know that New York thing. I've always said that Sid is an acquired taste. If you hang in, it's worth it.

I thought he went over the line many, many times, and I told him so. Ours was a very honest friendship. What I like about him—especially once he got down to Miami—is that he really had a show that was such a mixed bag. It was some of his crude takes on things, which are really unnecessary—I mean, *really* unnecessary.

After the Kylie Minogue comment, I don't think I spoke to him for six months. There's no need to be cruel. Funny is funny. When you go that route you're bordering on bully. It's sort of instinctive. And I bet he wrestled with that afterward. Look, the guy has a daughter. He has a fantastic wife. There's no way that Sid thought that way. We all wish we could take things back.

On the great side, his mind is always moving, and it's a very original, comprehensive mind. He's got a very, very alive intellect, and I've always really respected him about that. I think I know his heart. And he's actually so kind to people when he's with them.

We talked about me working with him. We have a great chemistry. I'm the type who could say to him, "Sid, your mother didn't raise you to talk like that." Instead of getting mad at him—and everybody gets mad at him—that's what I would say. "Sid, that is not nice." Am I dreaming? No. I think it could have been smart radio, not rude radio.

He's a complicated guy. Sometimes he's just his own worst enemy. He really is. There was nobody who thinks he doesn't do radio at a high level. There was just no reason for him to do some of the things he did. He has something going well and then he blows his leg off. Do you think he's just too late for his time? Remember all those people, those twisted geniuses—John Belushi and all those guys? He's a talent, he's a huge talent. Mike Francesa told me he wanted to hire Sid. You cannot get higher in radio in this country. Mike Francesa ruled it for what, 15 years? If Mike Francesa wanted to hand-pick Sid, that's how huge he is. I think talent is like a raft. You can't hold the raft underwater. It comes back up.

I think the title for this book is all wrong. *You're Wrong and You're Ugly*. That is just not right. You know what the book should be called? *My Inner Hamlet*. That's what he is. He's Hamlet. He's rash and he's impulsive. Of course Hamlet was a madman. And yet Hamlet questioned the world; he questioned himself. Hamlet had very intense emotions and in the end he was philosophical. That's what Sid really is.

If You're Buying, I'm Drinking…
and Drinking…and Drinking…

I'm a self-admitted alcoholic. I never try to hide it. I never got into trouble because of the drinking. It was the drinking that led to the other things that got me into trouble.

The first time I got really, really hammered was in the mountains in upstate New York, where my family goes every summer. We went to Ideal Bungalow Colony or Woodland Bungalow Colony until my parents bought a home in White Lake Homes. And we're still there, all these years later. I go up for three weeks every July. It's about six miles outside of Monticello, and it's a beautiful community. It's like a bungalow colony with a big pool, softball on Sundays and basketball on Saturdays, a casino, and a comedian and a singer who entertain on Saturday nights.

We started going up there when I was 11 years old. There were tons of families who went up there every summer like ours, and I grew up with all those guys, like 100 of 'em. We were teenagers, smoking pot together, and now we've all got kids. The house is exactly one mile away from Yasgur's Farm, the site of the Woodstock concert. When we were kids in the '80s, my buddies who drove would take the cars up to the hills, to Yasgur's Farm. We'd hang out there all night, drinking beer and smoking pot. Since then, they've built a beautiful thing up there called Bethel Woods. If you're into the whole Woodstock thing, it's a lovely museum. They have old videos, movies and music, and also a huge outdoor amphitheater. Every summer they have bands like Dave Matthews or Counting Crows come through, all on the grounds where they had the original Woodstock.

On Saturday nights the older kids used to go to a place at the Pines Hotel in South Fallsburg called the Chalet. The Chalet was an amazing place. It was so popular that I had buddies who would drive up from Brooklyn, and you're talking about a good two-and-a-half-hour trip. They would leave Brooklyn at like 7:30 PM on a freaking Saturday night, and they wouldn't get up there around 10:30. They were all doing coke and screwed up and drinking, so by the time they got up there they were ready to party. And when the place closed at 5:00 AM, they would drive back to Brooklyn. On Monday nights, for people who stayed up there during the summer, they had a huge thing called Mambo Night at the Raleigh Hotel. We'd drink and hang out there, too.

I was about 15 years old when I first went to the Chalet. My buddy Charlie Blecher drove me, and I got fucking annihilated. I had never really been drunk before, like really *drunk* drunk. I remember driving home. I threw up all over his car. I'm telling you, two, three weeks later they were still finding pieces of salad and carrots inside the fucking window. It was disgusting. That same summer that I threw up in Charlie Blecher's car. I threw up in my friend Bob Martin's Mercedes. I was new to drinking, and my friends kept taking me out every weekend. I'd get fucking blitzed, and I throw up in their cars. So sue me.

For most of my life, the drink of my choice has been Long Island iced tea. It's like everything else in my life: the more the merrier. I researched it very, very hard and could not find a drink that had more liquor in it than the Long Island iced tea. I believe there are seven altogether, when you include the liqueurs and the gin and the vodka and the rum and everything else. I knew that if

I had four or five of those, I'd be good to go. Then I'd have like eight, nine, or 10. If I had to, I'd drink straight vodka. When I was at the height of my drinking and drug abuse, I would go out all night into the city and drink iced teas and do coke all night and get back to my parents' house at like 6:00 in the morning. They'd be asleep, I'd be downstairs in the basement—I basically had my own apartment down there—and I'd raid the liquor cabinet and drink straight scotch or straight vodka.

I used to sleep downstairs on a couch that pulled out into a bed. After I finished the bottles of vodka and scotch, I'd stuff 'em inside the bed. My mother would clean my room every once in a while and find an empty bottle of scotch lodged in there! I actually stuck it inside the pillows, forgot about it, went out that day, and that was it. My parents were in complete denial. They knew what was going on. They knew I was coming home at 6:00 or 7:00 in the morning and partying like a madman, but they were in complete denial, up until the point when I finally went to rehab for the first time. They figured, *He's fucked up again, but what are you going to do?*

That's how the whole drinking started. There's nothing I can't drink. I have never been much of a beer guy. If I went to places where they only served beer and wine, I'd have to leave. There were certain times when I'd get home at 5:00 or 6:00 in the morning and walk down to Kings Highway in Brooklyn just to get a pack of cigarettes and a six-pack of beer (but never on Sundays, because they didn't sell beer on Sunday mornings, which really sucked). I would drink beer, but it was always a last resort. I prefer vodka, but I'd drink anything. I'd drink scotch, I'd drink rum, I'll drink gin, I'll drink whatever the fuck you have, but vodka is my beverage of choice. And it makes me laugh; they go, "What kind of vodka do you want?" I'm like, "Are you kidding me?" They'd go, "You want Skyy Vodka, you want Absolut Vodka, you want Stolichnaya, you want Grey Goose?"

Just give me the fucking vodka. I don't care if you give me Gordon's. Give me fucking vodka. I don't give a fuck. Those mornings at 6:00 AM, after a full night of drinking and cocaine, I'd be drinking warm fucking Gordon's vodka out of my parents' liquor cabinet—and it was in plastic bottles. It was fucking disgusting, but it didn't stop me.

To me, drinking was always the pregame. *I'm going to a bar now, and I need to put my big balls on.* I never drank just to get drunk. Drinking was the pregame so that I could get the confidence to do everything else—to score chicks, to get coke, all the real good stuff. But once I had a few drinks in me, I kept drinking, because I was up and I had to remain fucked up. I never looked forward to the drinking part. There's a story that the R&B singer Rick James went on a drug-fueled binge that kept him up for something like 10 days. I was up for four days once, back in 1990. My parents were away on vacation in Florida, and I was up four straight days without sleep, just fueled by cocaine and liquor. I drank the whole time. I had just gotten back from Florida and I looked great. I was tan and felt great and my parents were away. I went to the city on a Friday night to a place called Sing-Along, which must have been the first karaoke nightclub in Manhattan. Went out there with my buddies on a Friday night. Tuesday morning it finally stopped. I slept for a day and half after that.

The most I ever slept in one shot was in college at the University of Miami. I was up for three or four days also doing drugs, and then I ended up taking like a whole bottle of Quaaludes just to fall asleep. These were legitimate. I know you can't get the 714s any more, but this was 1985 and it was Miami. There were still pretty good pharmaceutical Quaaludes then. I was up for three or four days, and I had to get some sleep. I took like half a bottle and slept for two days, woke up, and pissed and shit myself. It was terrible. I've done that a couple of times. That's always a good time.

WE NOW INTERRUPT OUR REGULARLY SCHEDULED BROADCAST
FOR A WORD FROM...

SCOTT FERRALL, Sirius Satellite Radio

I'm on 8:00 PM to midnight on Stern 101. It's a cool gig. I get away with murder. I guess it's the perfect place for me. It's ridiculous what I get away with. When I was doing terrestrial radio I was always in trouble. I had three lawyers, and it was always nothing but problems. I went to Sirius, and now they high-five me when I'm doing my thing. It's great.

I first met Sid at WFAN in 1997 or 1998. I was working there from 1995 to 1999. I just did it from afar. I was in Los Angeles, fooling everyone. It was a New York show, it was a WFAN home station, and they would send me the *Post* and the *News* and the *Times* and *Newsday* every day via fax. I'd come into work, and there would be 3,000 sheets on the floor. My producers would organize them, and I'd turn it into a New York show at night. I'd come on after the Mets and Rangers and Knicks games and talk New York sports.

I would come in from Los Angeles about four times a year to do shows, mostly for MTV, and I met Sid when I came to New York a few times. One night Sid was there and eventually the program director, Mark Chernoff, was smart enough—I always thought he was smart—put us together on the air one night. I thought we were magical together. I really believe we would have been No. 1 in New York if they ever put us together. We would have been ruthless, and we would have had huge ratings together. I think he's funny and brilliant, and I think I'm crazy and I know my sports. You put a combination like that together, and it would have been a lot like *Mike and the Mad Dog*. There would have been a lot of success, but it never came to be.

The show I did with Sid was the show when I made fun of Doris from Rego Park's cancer, and that got me in all kinds of trouble. They made me apologize to her, which I thought was gay. I don't care about Doris from Rego Park. I worked for Mel Karmazin for a long time, and I offended a lot of people over the years. If I worried about one caller I offended, I'd never make it in New York or in this business. I have no feelings about making fun of people. I make fun of myself more than I make fun of people. Sid and I are one in the same—he's ruthless, and I'm capable of hurting feelings. I didn't know she had cancer! I'm from Los Angeles! I'd never heard of her. I'd never been in on the daytime saga that was WFAN. I just heard this woman coughing and hacking and I said, "Clear that shit out, honey," and it got me in all kinds of trouble. They said, "Apologize or you're fired." I was like, "All right, I'll apologize, but I'd rather be fired." They didn't believe me when I said I didn't know her. I was always the bad boy, but I did what they said so I wouldn't lose all my money.

I consider myself the outsider at WFAN; I considered myself the guy without a green card, like I was on a visa. I would come in and do shows and no one liked me, starting with Mike Francesa and Chris Russo. They would go on the air and talk about how they weren't going to work with me and then I'd finish No. 1 in nights in New York and that all shut up in a hurry. I never had anything against 'em. Once, I got tired of hearing them talk badly about me so I started taking shots at them. I've not liked Fatso ever since. But I respect Chris and like him. I think he's very good at what he does, and I'm glad he's at Sirius. I mean that. I still think he's not a big fan of mine. I think Chris feels threatened when guys come along, like at the FAN or here at Sirius. He wouldn't like Sid and me because we're outrageous, and he's supposed to be the outrageous guy. I have no animosity towards Chris. People think I do, and it's amazing how long something like that can linger. I've always been very nice to him and friendly, and I think people just assume I'm this bad guy and I just have to live with it. People think, *Ferrall is an asshole and he argues and fights with people.* I'm just a totally cool guy, a nerd. I have two kids and a beautiful family and wife and I just go home like anybody else. I love sports and I do a crazy show. I'm crazy, but I'm not out to get anybody.

I don't think it's a big secret that people in my business drink and party and do drugs. Anybody that thinks I'm in a religious business is imagining things. I know a lot of people who have the exact same afflictions as Sid. I've certainly partied, and I know all of my colleagues have partied. Sid's no different than anybody else—his stuff just went public. Essentially he's the guy driving the car who got pulled over with the bag of weed and said, "Dad, I've never done it before. This is the first time. But they found the bag of weed in my car, and oh my God, suddenly I'm a drug addict." I just think Sid got publicly embarrassed. I think he understands he's a renegade, he's a maverick. He's going to do things like that. He's no different than Howard Stern or Don Imus or me or anybody.

Most of my friends have been able to keep their demons in the closet. Sid obviously was unfortunate. I love him and I'm proud of him for fighting his demons. If people are going to judge you for the rest of your life because you've smoked some weed or did some blow or something, screw 'em.

I think people missed the chance to put us together. Not only could we have done it, we would have killed everyone, including Mike and the Mad Dog. We were younger, cooler, hipper, and we're not fat. I would have turned that into money. I would have made fun of Mike until I was No. 1, and he would have hated every minute of it. He thinks no one can beat him, and I used to crush him with numbers. He had a bigger audience because he was on in drive time. No one can beat the Pope in the afternoon, I get it, but if you look at pure numbers, I was getting a 10 share.

I think Mike is a very, very astute, smart man, a brilliant guy who does his thing, and he realized that Sid and him together would have been huge. Mike's great at what he does; I just think he's an asshole. I think he's a great talent that just treats people like shit; he always treated me like shit, and I don't like him. But I believe he's brilliant at what he does. I worked with the guy for four years. He hated my guts; that was obvious.

Sid was great with Imus, and he would have been even better with Francesa and CBS, because they're so corporate and so stuffed-shirt. I know all of 'em. I worked for them three times. They got nervous when Sid opened his mouth on my show, and they got nervous that he was going to be on with Mike. They made a big mistake. Sid will be No. 1 in Miami; it's just too easy of a market. Sid's too good not to be No. 1 in Miami. He'll own Miami. It's his.

Mike and the Mad Dog: the Underbosses of New York Radio

I've listened to *Mike and the Mad Dog* for a long time. I called in a couple of times as "Sid from Brooklyn." I wasn't a very memorable caller, so they probably don't remember. I was certainly a fan of those guys from way back. I still am. When they started in 1989, I was 21 years old. Those guys were the best. Every afternoon that was the only show I had on.

Their show had the perfect dynamic. In one guy you had Mike Francesa: the insider. He knew everybody—which is true, by the way. I think a lot of people out there feel as if Mike says that stuff but he doesn't talk to anybody. That's bullshit. I can tell you for a fact Mike does talk to the people he says he does. If he says, "I talked to Omar Minaya in my car," or "I talked to Bill Parcells," odds are he did. He was the inside guy, the laid-back guy. He knows everything. In the other guy, you had Chris Russo, "Dog," a maniacal fan who got overemotional at times, like most fans do. And I think that dynamic worked perfectly. Their styles were so different, and yet they both knew a heck of a lot. Both of them are very smart when it comes to sports.

Dog is actually a lot smarter than people give him credit for. He has always taken a beating that he's not that bright, but believe me, Dog can tell you who ran the football on 2nd-and-6 with eight minutes to go in the Ice Bowl. At the end of the day they were both kind of funny and both very smart, but they were so different in their delivery that they provided the perfect complement to one another. Listen, you can argue that part of the reason they broke up after 19 years is the same reason they had that monster success. Listeners like controversy, the yelling and the screaming and the disagreements, and Mike and Chris were great at that. It made for great radio. What it didn't make for was a great off-air relationship between the two of them, and when they finally broke up they had had enough of each other. They had made a lot of money together and they were realistic in knowing that they needed one another to get where they had to go. They might not have been able to stand the other guy, but they both knew what they meant to the other. That's why they showed up at 1:00 every day.

I had sort of a fiery relationship with both of them but especially Dog. One of the five or six most famous Dog rants is between him and me on the *Imus* show. I called him an overpaid, overrated, loudmouth scumbag—and a faggot for playing tennis. Imus frequently had Mike and Chris on, and Imus liked to make fun of them, even though Imus is actually very friendly with Mike Francesa off the air, certainly friendlier with Mike than he is with Chris.

At the end of the day, no matter what anybody tells you, Imus was the Godfather. He was Gotti, and Mike and Chris were like his top soldiers. That's the way it was. They were certainly very dangerous mobsters, don't get me wrong. Let's use *The Sopranos*. If Imus was Jimmy Gandolfini, then the other two guys were like Paulie Walnuts and Christopher. You don't want to fuck with 'em, but at the end of the day Imus was still Tony Soprano. If anybody else makes fun of Mike and Chris, like Joe Benigno, he gets whacked. When I was on the show, I had Imus' protection. For the most part Mike and Chris got it; they were cool when I made fun of them. But there were a few instances when they were upset. But Imus told them, "You know what, F— you. Leave my guy Sid alone." And at that point I became "his guy." He would always make it very, very clear that I was his guy, and they pretty much had to take it.

Imus did his thing, Mike and Chris did their thing, and there was a clear hierarchy there. It was those three guys, and then there was everybody else. For a couple of years there I was like fourth, if you considered the amount I got paid for *Imus* and for the midday show, all the responsibility I had, and the amount of time I was on the air. I may have been fourth, but the difference between those three guys and me was night and day. The feeling was palpable. There was a major superstar in the morning and two superstars in the afternoon. The joke was that the rest of the day was just filler. For me, it was a little different. I was part of the midday show, but I was also part of the *Imus* crew. It was like a mob crew; they had to deal with that shit.

For the most part we had a good relationship. Well, okay, Dog and I probably didn't. Dog felt that at times I was a bit too much. Dog's a pretty religious guy. He goes to church every Sunday. He's a pretty straightforward guy, and I'm just a bit too much for him. We had very similar styles in that we were both kind of ADHD, very frenetic and energetic. But we were still very different people. At times we had a good relationship, but we never had a great relationship.

Mike was different. The couple of times I upset him, he's always gotten it. Mike has actually been pretty supportive of me over the years. When things happened, he was one of the guys who would often go to Mark Chernoff or somebody else there and have my back. Mike and I have a much better relationship than Dog and I have. Actually, I wouldn't call my relationship with Dog bad. I would call it *nonexistent*. But I know for a fact that Mike respects me and my talent, and I certainly respect him and his talent. I would bust their balls and say, "You guys are just in the right place at the right time, and if I was there 20 years ago I would have the same success," and I'm not sure at times I didn't mean that. At the end of the day I certainly respected what they had accomplished.

For most of the guys at FAN, there isn't much jealousy. They knew coming in that there was Imus and there was Mike and Chris. I was jealous because I have a very inflated sense of self. I understand why Imus is the legend that he is, like Stern and Mike and the Mad Dog. I don't resent them and would never say that they don't deserve it, but I've always felt that I'm every bit as good. At times, I think I'm better. Dog is great at a lot of things, but there are plenty of things that I do better. Most guys come in there, and they're just so happy to be working at WFAN. They know those three guys are the superstars. And maybe if I had just done the middays and the Giants I would have felt that way. But because I had the *Imus* experience and got accolades from some of the biggest people in the business, people who would tell me, *there's nobody in that place that has as much or more talent than you*, I started to believe it. I really felt like, *Hey, why can't I have some of that?* It was less about the money for me and more about just the respect.

One of the things I like about Mike is you kind of get the same Mike every single day. A lot of people tend to think he's obnoxious, he's arrogant, or he doesn't give a crap. My personal experience with Mike has shown me that he's a really good guy. I am aware of things he has done for me off the air and I am aware of things he has done for other people. He has gone above and beyond for some of his coworkers at FAN and some of his friends.

I know for a fact Mike has done a lot more nice things for me and for other people at FAN than Dog has. Dog was just, to me, phony. One day Dog acted like he loved me, like he was my best friend, and the next day I didn't even exist. All I want is for somebody to be consistent. Mike was a lot more consistent. The funny thing is, people out there tend to prefer Dog. To listeners, Dog has the better attitude. He's always laughing, and he's funny and gregarious when he meets you. He's got a big laugh and a smile, but at the end of the day Dog is also the guy that just wants to play tennis up in Connecticut with his millionaire friends, and get his good seats for Bruce Springsteen. Mike is real, and Dog is a lot like his character.

He never said this to me, but people often told me, "Dog feels like you're ripping off his act." Granted, I was probably the closest thing to Dog that FAN had—on the air at least. I was similarly excitable, I suppose. But he's a guy who goes to church on Sundays and lives in his nice little town up in Connecticut and lives a charmed life, He always has, going back to his college days at Rollins. I'm a guy who's been through the ringer. I put myself through it, don't get me wrong—the drugs, the alcohol, the gambling. We may have been brought up similarly, but we've lived very different lives the last 15 to 20 years. But yeah, on the *Imus* show they used to tease me all the time, "Of course Dog doesn't like you. You're trying to steal his act!"

Jealousy is a tough word. I often say I'm jealous of people who I don't think have talent but who have done better than me. I think Dog has talent, but if you're asking me if I was there in 1989 when they started this thing, assuming I had no off-the-field problems, would I have had the same success in those shoes, then the answer is yes. No doubt about it. At the end of the day, I might be like Dog but maybe even a better version. I know sports just like he does. I know Springsteen, the music, like he does. But Dog is pretty limited. As a sports guy he's terrific. I'll even go as far to say I don't think Dog gets the credit sometimes for the amount of sports he knows. People often say, "Mike is the guy who knows everything, and Dog is kind of the clown act." Not true. But Dog is limited outside of that stuff. You can't have an intelligent conversation with Dog about politics. He won't be able to tell you what's happening on *Lost* or *American Idol*. He doesn't care. That's fine. He'll stay up watching the San Francisco Giants at midnight while I'm watching what everyone else will talk about the next day. It was fine, because Dog's role at WFAN for 20 years was the same. But I think now that he's doing his Sirius stuff, he's not going to have a choice. If it lasts and he has a lengthy stay on that thing, I think he's going to have to broaden his horizons.

After Dog left FAN to start up his own channel on Sirius, I e-mailed Dog's program director, Steve Torre, for a couple of days about getting me on the show. Dog doesn't even call me back. I e-mailed Dog incessantly and sent him texts when he first started. I was like "Doggie, c'mon man, it's a brand-new channel." I already had my job down in Miami, so I wasn't looking for a full-time gig. I was basically looking to do some weekends, some fill-in stuff. I figured he was with a new channel, so he needed to get another big name on that channel. He hasn't done that, by the way. He's put a bunch of guys around him that no one ever fucking heard of. I think some of that is money. Dog got all $15 million and probably left about $1.50 for everybody else. But the other part of it is ego. He doesn't want to share the spotlight.

I went to New York to visit with some guys over at Sirius because they were thinking of doing a show with me and Lawrence Taylor, which would have been great. We visited with Steve Cohen and Sirius president Scott Greenstein. Sure enough, I bump into Dog in the bathroom. There's Dog again, slapping me on the ass, "Hey, I'm not mad at you. I did want to talk to you. I've been busy. I lost my voice." He had more fucking excuses than Jimmy Carter's got liver pills. So we went into his office, and we have a nice little conversation for about half an hour. I said to him, "Dog, here's what I'm proposing: a couple of weekends, maybe a couple of shows from the Super Bowl. I'm not looking for a lot of money." He said, "You know what, I love the idea. Let's talk more about it." He claimed he couldn't do anything on a full-time basis for two reasons: first, the money and second—and this is unbelievable—he claimed I was a little too out of the box. I'm thinking to myself, *Dog, you're on fucking Sirius Satellite, Howard Stern's station. What do you mean* I'm *out of the box?* He wanted to maintain this conservative sports deal. He didn't want to get too crazy. But in the meantime, he had Artie Lange on live from the Springsteen concert talking about masturbating. Out of the box? You mean to tell me the name Sid Rosenberg is not going to help you get a couple of listeners on a station that is brand new? Dog never got back to me, never called me again, kind of left me in the lurch. I'm not going to lie. To this day I'm still pissed about it.

Then again, it wasn't like Dog and I didn't have good times together. We had one night at Jim Fassel's house with our wives. We had a great time that night. And then there was a time when Dog and I played Joseph Abboud and Patrick McEnroe in Abboud's annual charity golf and tennis tournament. Dog and I played together, and that was a blast. He also gave me his Bruce Springsteen concert tickets, and Danielle and I went. It was *The Rising* tour.

I still maintain that the reason why I had popularity in New York and one of the reasons why I still do was even though I had some real controversial things and some nasty things and some pretty public fuckups, was that a lot of the average guys out there could relate to what I've gone through my whole life. The majority of the listening audience can't relate to waking up at 8:00 AM in a multimillion dollar house in the Hamptons and playing tennis. Nobody wants to hear some rich guy talking over the airwaves. On the last show they had, when Chris thanked Mike for all of the success they shared, he could have just said, "I never would have been as successful and enjoyed all this without you." Instead, he rattled off all the things that he acquired along the way.

WE NOW INTERRUPT OUR REGULARLY SCHEDULED BROADCAST
FOR A WORD FROM…

CHRIS RUSSO, Former WFAN cohost,
Mike and the Mad Dog, Mad Dog Radio, Sirius XM

Down deep, Sid's got a good heart. I think Sid's a decent person. He would take the shirt off his back for you. Sid cares; Sid can emote. How that translates into how he lives his life is a different situation. He makes mistakes, he's misguided, he gets carried away, and he has all those issues. Down deep I do think Sid cares, so he's salvageable. I wouldn't lend money to him. I don't know if I trust him with taking care of my four kids at night. But overall I think Sid's a decent human being. In a lot of ways I look at him as a lost soul.

Sid's a very knowledgeable sports guy. Instead of just doing his thing and letting people discover Sid, Sid wants you to make sure you discover him—and that gets him in trouble. He's so wrapped up in being on *Inside Edition,* he's so starved for attention, that he misses the big picture. The big picture is: Sid, go on the air, do a talk show or do *Imus* three or four hours a day, do a good job with it, be enthusiastic, show that you care, show you have passion, and somebody will discover you.

He wears his ethnicity on his sleeve, and that gets him in trouble. It would be like a Christian freak going on the air and saying "God" every five seconds. The whole world knows Sid's Jewish, and I just don't think anybody cares. Do a sports show! I have a lot of friends who've said that to me over the years, both Christian and Jewish friends, that Sid sometimes gives you that ethnicity angle. It gets a little overbearing.

I never thought he was trying to rip off my style. I know people think that. People think that Sid and I didn't like each other. Sid has propelled that as well. Never true. People are going to say, "Russo's lying." It doesn't bother me. I go on the air and I do the show and I don't pay too much attention to what people at other stations are doing. I never once ever went in to correct Sid on the air or said, "You sound too much like me. You're trying to be too much like me." I never gave it a whole heck of a lot of thought. Now, Sid and I had our issues, we fought on topics but as far as Sid trying to be me—I'm sure people at FAN would say, "Russo, I don't trust him." It never bothered me.

Did I take Sid that seriously when he was screaming and yelling and calling me a fag because I played tennis? I did not. When he went to Miami, I did an interview with him. I went on for about 20 to 25 minutes. I was very impressed how well he did that interview. Sid is a good interviewer, he knows sports, but he just lets crazy things get in the way sometimes. Sid doesn't understand that there is a degree of accountability when you go on the radio on a day-to-day basis, and obviously he loses sight of that. Going on with *Imus*, which doesn't rate accountability that seriously, is very dangerous. Sid goes off the deep end, and you can't trust him personally sometimes with all the issues. He's got the demons flying around, and then you put him with Imus, who goes crazy on those demons—that's a very bad combination. I used to tell that to FAN all the time: you're giving Imus a guy for shock effect who will take things too far because he's not ready to handle that. FAN didn't care, because all FAN wanted was to get that shock effect and make *Imus* be more listenable, and as a result that caused lots of trouble. He couldn't handle that kind of responsibility, and I blame FAN there as much as I blame Sid.

They used him. That's a very poor job by our company at the time. They put him in certain spots, and then when he went off the deep end they couldn't believe it. What did you expect? He's got to wake up at 4:30 AM, he's got to try to be funny, and he's got to react to what Imus says. He and Bernie [McGuirk] with the stupid fight, the boxing match they had. You put Sid in these situations and you might get a little bang for your buck out of it, but you're also going to be in a spot where you're going to be embarrassed. That's as much FAN's fault as Sid's fault. He gave Bernie a foil, which was important. He was a young-sounding voice, which they needed. Sid had a role. He could be a good talk show host. But the seven hours on the air was too much responsibility for a guy who had this many demons flying around. It's almost like they wanted to soak the rag up as much as they could, and then they were shocked when Sid went off the deep end.

The problem with Sid, to me, is that he gets mixed up with things that don't serve him well. Sid tries too hard to be a celebrity. When you try too hard to be a celebrity, it always backfires. I don't care about that crap. How many times have you seen me at the Super Bowl running out to a freaking Playboy party? How many times have you seen me stay out until 2:00 in the morning? Do I ever come in staggering from the night before? I'm not in the same group of guys as Sid.

I know Sid and Joe [Benigno] tried to tweak us occasionally. I thought they were too New York. They were not for everybody's taste, Joe and Sid. We considered bringing him in here at Sirius, but you can't trust Sid. He might think I did that because I don't like him. That's not true. You got me on the air, him on the air—it's almost too New York. And I couldn't trust Sid to do 6:00–10:00 AM Monday through Friday in this kind of format. He wanted in and I like Sid and he's got ability, but he tries too hard for chrissake. Sid, sit back, let us make a decision. He was driving me crazy. I didn't feel two months into this I could go out there and bring Sid in. He had issues at FAN, the QAM thing in Miami. I just thought it was a little too soon. The timing wasn't proper. It wasn't a personality thing, it wasn't like, "I'll be damned if I'm gonna hire Sid and let him take over my stage." That never crossed my mind.

I think Sid and I have a decent relationship. I think Sid likes me down deep; I like Sid down deep. I think FAN made a mistake, giving him too much responsibility. It's like having Josh Hamilton of the Reds or Texas. You can't throw him into the big spots that quickly. You have to break him in.

Another thing about Sid, he's in Miami, and his main goal in life is to get to New York. Do good shows in Miami, for chrissake. Sid's never happy. Sid is always striving. Have you ever noticed that? I do this job, but I want to do that job. I do this job, but I have to do that job. He wants too much. Just do the job that you have.

I don't think CBS would have taken the chance of Sid coming in to replace me at FAN. Mike [Francesa] knows, if you're going to get somebody to replace me, you got to bring somebody in there who's not like me. He would have been careful giving that to Sid, almost like it's a poor representation of trying to replace me with Sid. I think Mike likes Sid. He feels bad for Sid in some ways.

If you want to tell me 20 years ago if Sid started with Mike, if you want to tell me in 1989, you reverse it so that Sid was 28 then just like I was 28, if you put Sid with Mike then, could he have lasted 19 years? I don't know about the demons. You have to handle the role and the responsibility. I think that would have gone to his head and gotten him in some trouble. As far as the actual show is concerned, could he have kept up with Mike, could he have added an element to it, could that have been a decent listen? You could definitely argue that.

[]

WE NOW INTERRUPT OUR REGULARLY SCHEDULED BROADCAST
FOR A WORD FROM…

MIKE FRANCESA, Former cohost,
Mike and the Mad Dog, WFAN; Host, *Mike'd Up*, WFAN and WNBC-TV

I know Sid's deal was to try to be outrageous. Sid was obviously someone who wanted to, without question, make a splash, which was clear. I think Sid has some ability. He's a guy who can do a show and he can be entertaining, and obviously he can get himself in a mess. I always got along well with him. I always liked Sid personally. I always thought he was harmless, and that he was trying to be outrageous. I like Sid. Some people didn't.

I never really got into a position where I had to protect Sid. A couple of times when he got in trouble he came and asked me for advice. Sid was really more aligned with Imus than he was with me, so if he needed help, he usually went to Imus. There have been times since Sid left when I've tried to give him some advice when he's called and asked. It's not like I ever hung out with him. I don't socialize with him. I don't even know the depth of Sid's issues. It's not my business. I wasn't around Sid. Dog [Chris Russo] and I didn't even socialize together. I never socialize with guys from the station. First of all, they were never in the same place as me, and I always felt like most of them were younger than me. Plus I just didn't make it a habit. I never saw Sid in the social setting; I never saw him out of control or anything. I never saw any of that stuff. I've heard the stories about him not showing up and disappearing and all that stuff. Dog and I really kept ourselves pretty much removed from that stuff. Our show was very insulated from the other shows, always has been.

I did know Sid and Dog didn't really like each other very much. Sid attacked Dog—he went after Dog a lot on the air. He didn't come after me very much but he went after Dog a lot, and that's why there was an animosity there that I kind of sensed. I know he and Craig Carton didn't get along. I know Don Imus always liked him, and I always liked him. I never had a reason not to like him. He never did anything to annoy me or bother me. He was always very good to me, always very nice to me, always very complimentary. Sid never gave me a hard time.

Dog didn't talk much about Sid. Sid used to say if he were put with me instead of Dog that he'd be as successful as Dog was, which was something I know Dog wasn't very happy about. Sid was just looking to do anything he could do to basically elevate his position. Sid desperately wants to be a star. He desperately wants to be an important personality. He has obviously been trying to do that for a very long time. He has struggled dramatically in a lot of ways. I do wish him well.

Sid's always going to be able to get a job. People like him on the air. He's entertaining; he can be outrageous. There's a role for a guy like that on the air—there's no question. He fit in well with what Don wanted him to do. Obviously Sid was in the wrong place at the wrong time with the [Rutgers] thing. I'm sure he feels like collateral damage.

Personally, you don't know in life who you're going to like and not like. I always liked Sid. From the first time I met him I liked him. There were times when I realized he had really screwed up and had really done some things that made no sense, and he deserved to take whatever he was going to take for it. But I also always thought there was a redeeming value to Sid. Sid is fortunate that, for some reason, people don't stay angry at him. He plays the victim well. I do know plenty of people I worked with who really didn't like him for a variety of reasons, but I've always found that people pretty much didn't stay angry at him. You understand his shortcomings. I think people find Sid and his act very different and very amusing. It's almost like a role Bill Murray would have played in an old *Saturday Night Live* sketch. He's almost playing that guy who comes into the room who is trying too hard. Everyone knows he's full of it, but people for some reason are going to laugh at it. They're going to get a kick out of him.

Sid has always tried to make himself more important than he really is. There's something funny about that. Other people, you'd be like, "What an idiot." And you do say, "What an idiot" to Sid, but for some reason it's amusing with him. Just the fact Sid's still working…a lot of guys don't get 10 chances, and he's had something like 10 chances. There are some individuals who people want to rehabilitate and will take the time to rehabilitate. Why? I have no reason. Some people, they want to be done with them immediately. Other people, they want to see if they can fix them. People have wanted to take the time to fix Sid. I think that's his blessing. Part of his blessing is he has whatever that quality is. He doesn't make people just discard him. I don't think they take him all that seriously. They realize that Sid thinks it's an act and that Sid thinks, a lot of times, that what he's doing is a goof, and you're going to think it is, too. It is harmless, except for him sometimes saying some really offensive, stupid things, which we all know he said. I understand the people who have been outraged with him. It's crazy to say it, but I don't think he really means it when he says it. You just think he shot his mouth off again.

It helps him that people don't take him seriously. If they took him seriously I think he probably would have been discarded a while ago. Look at Mark Chernoff. He gave him more chances than anybody. Cherny went a long way to try to fix Sid. If Sid owes anybody a real debt of gratitude, it's Chernoff. He really went the extra mile, much more than anybody else. He really put his reputation on the line for Sid. I think that was almost like a father-son relationship there with those two. That's how I would explain it.

The New York Knicks, Sports Equivalent of the Girl with the Curl

I was born in 1967, so I can't go on and on about the days of Willis Reed and Walt "Clyde" Frazier and Dave DeBusschere and Phil Jackson. I was two years old in '69, and I was six when they won it with Earl "the Pearl" Monroe in 1973. My Knicks memories really start with those bad teams with Edmund Sherod, Rory Sparrow, Larry Demic, DeWayne Scales, Len "Truck" Robinson, and those guys. Of course, Bernard King was my favorite player ever. And then we had Marvin Webster and Bill Cartwright. And when we got Patrick Ewing, that was it—that's when I became a die-hard Knicks fan.

My first favorite player for the Rangers was Ron Duguay. My first favorite players for the Giants were all linebackers. Offensively, the first player I ever fell in love with was Rob Carpenter. For the Knicks, it was Bernard and then Patrick. But something happened along the way because I loved Micheal Ray Richardson. It's funny, my three favorite players of all time in New York are Lawrence Taylor, Darryl Strawberry, and Micheal Ray Richardson. Of course, they're all fucking bust-out cokeheads. That's what we all have in common. But that's about it. I loved that backcourt for the Knicks with Micheal Ray Richardson and Ray Williams.

Micheal Ray Richardson was better than flamboyant—he was tremendous. If he wasn't all fucked up, he could have been one of the great point guards. I'm telling you, he was that good. As it turned out, he went to Italy and became like the all-time leading scorer in European history. Unlike Lawrence Taylor and Darryl Strawberry, who at least were able to play, Micheal was so deep into coke that he couldn't play, he was so fucked up. He went to the Nets, and he was great. I became a Nets fan. Look, I love the Rangers, hate the Islanders; love the Mets, hate the Yankees; love the Giants, hate the Jets; but I root for the Knicks and the Nets. I became fans of both, because at one point Micheal Ray Richardson and Ray Williams became the backcourt for the Nets! They had that team with Micheal Ray and Ray Williams—along with Albert King, Darryl Dawkins, Foots Walker, Darwin Cook, and Mike O'Koren. I loved that team, and I actually started splitting my allegiances between the Knicks and the Nets. When I left New York in 2005 and I was living in Tenafly, New Jersey, I went to lots of Nets games with Vince Carter and Jason Kidd.

I've been to a lot of Knicks games. What are you going to say? I went through all the nonsense in 1994 with the Rockets, when the Knicks lost the championship. I was watching along with everybody else as O.J. Simpson and the white Bronco crept down the highway on TV during the NBA Finals. When they lost in the Finals to San Antonio in 1999, I was already living in Florida. That was the team that Ernie Grunfeld built with Marcus Camby and Latrell Sprewell. They ended up as the eight seed and made the Finals—and they fired Grunfeld for it! Ewing was healthy enough to beat Miami. He was still healthy enough to beat up on Alonzo Mourning. But he didn't play in the San Antonio series, and the Spurs had a young Tim Duncan, David Robinson, Sean Elliott, and Avery Johnson—and they killed the Knicks. Jeff Van Gundy put that team together, and the next thing you know they're in the NBA Finals.

I loved Pat Riley. I have a very nice relationship with Riley in Miami. As the president of the Heat, he's been great to me. He comes on my show all the time. He does a lot of radio shows in the south Florida area. He's very media savvy and does all the shows in an effort to promote Heat basketball. When he comes on with me, we talk politics and we talk Springsteen. Once I had Riley on, and I called "Little Steven" Van Zandt, who's a friend of mine. I said "Listen, Pat Riley's going to be on the phone." He knows Riley. Riley has been backstage at Springsteen concerts. So I asked Steven, "Do me a favor. I'm going to have him on, and about midway through the interview, if you don't mind, I'm going to tell him that somebody wants to say hello." Riley and Van Zandt had a back-and-forth for about five minutes. It was great.

I loved Riley as a coach, but when he sent a fax with his resignation, after his team went to the Finals, I was furious. Growing up in New York, I wasn't old enough to enjoy Red Holzman. My favorite coach was Jeff Van Gundy. For me it was always Jeff Van Gundy; him climbing onto Alonzo Mourning's leg is an indelible image. To me, he was just a gutty fighter. That's why Van Gundy is my favorite Knicks coach.

The Knicks gave us the Finals in 1994 and 1999. They never won a championship, but that never really bothered me as a Knicks fan. I often argue with the people in Miami, would you rather go 4–12 for 10 straight years and win one Super Bowl, or would you rather have the Dan Marino years? You win 11 games every season, go to the playoffs, even the AFC Championship Game, and throw for 5,000 yards every year. In short, you were relevant. As long as Patrick Ewing was there, the Knicks were relevant. They were in the Finals. They were in the playoffs. We had great rivalries with Michael Jordan and the Bulls and Hakeem Olajuwon and the Rockets. Everybody kills John Starks for his Game 7 against the

Rockets when he shot 2 of 18, but everybody forgets that, if not for John Starks in Game 6, there never would have been a Game 7. I think Starks gets a bad break there because he was so great in Game 6. He was awful in Game 7, and a lot of people, to this day, still think Riley made a huge mistake, that he should have gone with Rolando Blackman over John Starks, but Riley went with the guy who got him there. At least they were relevant. When they were relevant, I wasn't angry with the Knicks' organization when they didn't win. I wanted to win, but I knew Jordan was the best. And at the end of the day, as great at Patrick was, Hakeem was better.

I was on the air in New York when they traded Ewing to Seattle in the deal that brought Glenn Rice to the Knicks, and I just blasted Knicks fans, telling them they were going to be sorry about this. Guys were complaining at the end of Ewing's stay, guys like Larry Johnson and Latrell Sprewell, complaining that Patrick was starting to slow them down, that they could run with all these guys and they had to wait until the old Ewing gets down the end of the court to slow down the offense and get him the ball. I told them, "You're going to miss those days." And I was right.

Did Ewing miss the finger roll against Indiana? Yes. Did he make predictions (unlike Joe Namath or Mark Messier) that he didn't deliver on? Yes. But he is still one of the 10 best centers in the history of the game—and he made basketball relevant in New York for years! He never had a good team around him. I mean, c'mon—he went to the Finals with guys like Charles Oakley and Anthony Mason and John Starks. The '99 team had some talent with Sprewell, Camby, and Larry Johnson. But the team that went to the Finals in 1994: what the fuck was that? Really, even if Hakeem wasn't better than Patrick (and he was), Hakeem had Robert Horry, Vernon Maxwell, Sam Cassell, and Otis Thorpe around him.

If you look at the guys who played around Patrick during his stay in New York, it was garbage. Mark Jackson was a nice player who had a lot of assists. Derek Harper was at the end of his career. and so was Doc Rivers. He never had the guys around him. He wasn't going to be Jordan or Hakeem, he wasn't as good as David Robinson, but he never had the guys around him to win a championship. Never, ever. And I don't hold that against Patrick. In fact, I miss those days. I know Mike D'Antoni and Donnie Walsh will turn it around, and we're all praying to God that we get LeBron James in 2010. Fat chance. The last years with Dave Checketts were a mess. The other clown, Scott Layden, was a disaster. And then the biggest disaster of them all: Isiah Thomas. I miss those Ewing years, big time. We made the playoffs a couple of years ago when Isiah got Stephon Marbury. He and Keith Van Horn played well together, which was not the case in New Jersey. They got swept by the Nets. At least they made the playoffs.

Say what you want about the Giants and the Jets, but when the Knicks are good—and I know it's been a long time—they're the third most important team in the city. It's the Yankees, the Mets, and then the Knicks, I am convinced of that. I know the Giants have a great history, too. People always say that center field for the Yankees and quarterback for the Giants is as big as it gets, but I am convinced baseball and the Knicks are the biggest thing in the city, when the Knicks are good. There are still a bunch of people who go to the Garden now to see the Knicks, but man, you can't fucking watch 'em these days. Considering the product they put out, it's amazing they draw anybody at all. It's still, as Jordan said, the Mecca. There's no place in the world to watch a basketball game like Madison Square Garden. I don't care if the fucking Lakers win 90 championships. The Staples Center is nice, but it's nothing like the Garden.

WE NOW INTERRUPT OUR REGULARLY SCHEDULED BROADCAST
FOR A WORD FROM...

PAT RILEY, President, Miami Heat,
enshrined in Naismith Memorial Basketball Hall of Fame, 2008

I've talked to Sid a number of times over the years, and I find him very refreshing, gregarious, outgoing, at times over the top but at times incredibly forthright in what he does. It's fun to get on the show with him. He's a Brooklyn guy. I can sense that right from the get-go. They have a certain cachet about them, a *savoir New York faire* you could call it. He had *it*, and it's right straight in your face.

He really surprised me one time I went on with him. Sid brought on Steve Van Zandt from Springsteen's E Street Band. It was the old underground garage band routine. I've met Steve Van Zandt a number of times at the shows. I don't profess to be a dear, close friend of any of the band members. I know them like a lot of fans do, because I've just followed them over the years. I've had some good conversations with Steve, and it was a surprise. It was wonderful that Sid had him on. Van Zandt basically said, "OK, I'll get on, and I'll bust Riley's chops." That's what it was. I can remember him setting me up. Sid was saying, "I'm going to find out if Riley really knows any of these guys. Does he get behind stage, does he get in their locker room, does he talk to them, or is it all bullshit?" It was a great thing, an out-of-the-box type thing, and we had a lot of fun with it.

They say he's a sports talk show host, but he has that absolute reservoir of knowledge across the board. There is a lot of subject matter that he can speak to and in which he's very well versed, and I think that reservoir of knowledge is something that comes out at any time. He's got the spontaneity. A show that can go from pick-and-rolls to the military or Afghanistan or to whatever is a very enlightening experience.

Those of us who have been in the game a long time don't have a problem with direct criticism if there's logic and thought behind it. Criticism for the sake of criticism is a popular thing to do, and we sort of let it roll off our shoulders. We laugh at it. We hardly even address it. If I ever got onto a show with somebody who simply wanted to criticize for the sake of criticizing, then it would probably end up being some kind of bloodbath because my rationale vs. their rationale simply wouldn't fly. With Sid, there's logic and there's knowledge. He understands the salary cap, he understands trades, understands the balance of a roster and what you can and can't do, timing, all these things. If there is something that was negative about the game the night before, a substitution pattern or a play-set call or whatever, yeah, you can deal with that as a coach. If there was something that was said about a horrible trade that didn't work out, and he went back and really researched it across the board and dug down deep into it philosophically and numerically and salary cap then yeah, I would take that. But most people don't. That's why he's so well versed. So when he does get on you a little bit ,he's got a point, and I can argue that point with him without it becoming emotional.

I know Sid has had his problems. He's been honest about them and opened up his heart to them, and that's what allows you to grow. The highest form of sanity is change. Unless you change the way you go about doing things, those things you do are never going to change.

Jerry Seinfeld Told Me to Buzz Off, So What?

I got a call one day in 2004 from some girl named Christine from DreamWorks Animation out in Los Angeles. I thought maybe Don Imus was playing a joke on me or something. On the message she left she said Jerry Seinfeld was interested in having me a play a part in his upcoming movie. I was thinking, *C'mon, this has got to be a bunch of bullshit. Who's fucking with me today?*

I thought it was far-fetched, but I knew that Seinfeld was a fan of the FAN. He's been good friends, no overstatement, with Steve Sommers for years and years, and he goes on Sommers' show all the time. He's a die-hard Mets fan, and I'm a Mets fan. Sommers and I have a good relationship. So I'm thinking that he probably is aware of my work—but it's a stretch, even if he knows who I am, that he wants me to play a part in his movie.

I called Christine, and she says that he's coming out with an animated movie, *Bee Movie*. He's looking for voice guys for parts in the movie, and he likes my work. She asked me to meet him at some studio in midtown Manhattan to read for one of the parts. No shit. So I say, "Yeah, shit yeah, great, thanks."

My agent, Mark Lepselter, and I show up at the studio in midtown Manhattan one afternoon, and sure enough, there are bagels and stuff laid out, and whaddyaknow, there's Jerry Seinfeld with like two or three of his people. So I went to Seinfeld and said, "I know you're familiar with Steve Sommers, but I had no idea you were familiar with me." It turns out that he had listened to *Imus* that morning and he repeated something that I had said on *Imus* a couple of days before, so I knew he was listening to the show.

He said he liked my accent, that real fast, staccato Brooklyn accent. He thought I would be good for the movie. I was like, "Wow, this is great. I love your show. You're one of my all-time favorites. I'm just thrilled to be here." We went into the studio, and we were in there for over an hour. He had me read for the part of a hornet. He had me raise my voice high; he had me make my voice deep and low, all kinds of different ranges that I didn't even know I had with my voice. I think I read for two or three different parts—the hornet was supposed to be the nemesis for the bee in this movie. There were three different hornets, and I think I read for all three different parts.

It went really well. He kept saying, "You're perfect for this, you're perfect for this." When we were done I actually said to him, "Am I going to be in this movie?" I still didn't believe it at that point, you know? He was like, "You were great, you were great! Yeah, you're going to be in the movie. Why wouldn't you be in the movie? You were great!" He said, "We'll be in touch. We're going to bring some other people in and read some other parts and stuff, but you were great. You couldn't have been any better." So I left.

They were supposed to pay me scale, which at the time was $720, for that reading. Instead, they paid me double scale. They told me that Jerry was so happy with the way I read and the way everything went that they paid me $1,440 instead of $720. I'm thinking, *They paid me double scale. I got the part.* Seinfeld was just filled with superlatives. Everything I did he was just laughing. I mean, I was making Seinfeld laugh! Fuck, he's Jerry Seinfeld, he's supposed to make *me* laugh, and I spent an hour making *him* laugh. I was really under the impression that I was going to be in this movie.

I went on *Imus*, and I said, "I'm going to be in Jerry Seinfeld's movie." I kept calling Los Angeles to speak to this girl again, but I never got in touch with her again. I kept checking IMDB.com, the Internet Movie Database, to see when it was coming out and if they had the whole cast filled out. I really did fully expect to see my name attached to the movie. The thing comes out like a year later, and there's all these huge names, and I'm reading up and down the IMDB and I don't see my name. I'm frantic. I couldn't find Christine in Los Angeles, and obviously I don't have a number for Jerry Seinfeld, so I'm going back and forth with Steve Sommers. "Do me a favor, please contact Jerry for me," because at that point I'm already down in Florida. I've got Sommers going back and forth with Seinfeld, and eventually Sommers relays the message that Jerry thought I was great, but you know what, they decided not to use the character but he looked forward to maybe doing something down the road. Basically, I was left on the cutting room floor before I ever got there.

So I was never a hornet. That could have been the beginning of something huge. But hey, I'm still a Jerry Seinfeld fan. No hard feelings. Just hanging out with Jerry for over an hour in that studio that day—that was a thrill of a lifetime.

A Fresh Start

I came down to Florida in 1996. I've been in rehab twice in my life, the first time in 1995, and again 10 years later in 2005. In 1995, after I went to rehab for the first time, when my 30 days were up, they said to me, "You probably shouldn't go back to your old haunts in New York. You're 30 days clean; you're going in the right direction, why don't you go somewhere and go to a halfway house?" I have family in Florida and I have a house in Florida, so I came down to Boca Raton in 1995 to a halfway house.

I had not worked for a couple of months. I was working for my dad when I left New York in 1995. So I got a job waiting tables at L&N Seafood at the Boca Town Center Mall. I really had no direction. My next-door neighbor at the time, a guy by the name of Elan Baknin, had started with this company in Woodline. He's a Long Island kid, and we had played basketball together. He said, "I work at this company, it's on the Internet, and we've got 65,000 pages about sports."

I knew nothing about the Internet in 1995. I literally asked him what he was talking about. But he got me a job in customer service. I was like a guy at a brokerage firm who did the cold-calling. I'd get a list of people to call and say, "I know you're a New York Giants fan. Imagine 12,000 pages on the Internet about the New York Giants," and I would sell people the product. The boss walked down the aisle one day and said, "You know everything about sports. Why don't you try doing radio for us?" I didn't care. I wanted the money. It sounded like fun. So for the first time in my life, I was working in radio. It was 1997, and I was working for a guy named Scott Kaplan. It was an Internet radio show, and we had about six or seven listeners, I think. We had a guy in Australia, a guy in Germany, servicemen who understood you could get radio on the Internet. An auspicious start, perhaps, but that was how I broke into the business.

WE NOW INTERRUPT OUR REGULARLY SCHEDULED BROADCAST FOR A WORD FROM...

MIKE LEVY, Founder, SportsLine

I guess I gave Sid his start in radio.

We were just getting ready to launch our SportsLine site in August of '95. During that summer, we were getting everything ready to go, so we hired a customer service department because we were signing people up for our service. People were having trouble registering, and we had to have customer service to advise them and help them through the process. Sid was one of our first hires.

Sid didn't have a radio background. He was doing customer service. The Internet was brand new, and people were having trouble with their connections and with their browsers and all kinds of stuff. People were having trouble logging onto the service or entering our contests. They would call in and have a guy like Sid walk them through the process.

We had decided early on that we wanted to go into radio on the Internet, and we were one of the first to do it. We brought in a radio consultant, and we looked at all the local sports radio talent. Of course we didn't want to pay top dollar. We ended up getting a guy from WQAM in Miami: Scott Kaplan. Scott was on like the midnight shift. I used to listen to WQAM, and I'd never even heard of Scott Kaplan.

We decided to see if there was anybody internally that could be a sidekick for Scott. We went through the whole thing, and he it turned out Sid had such tremendous sports knowledge, he had a great personality, and could really fit in well with Scott. So we gave him a chance ,and it turned out to be a big success. The guys were a great team. Almost every day there was something these guys came up with. They would figure out something to say that was funny about almost everybody that they interviewed. I'd say their show was probably more entertaining than anything I've ever heard on sports talk radio since. I felt, after that show launched, those guys were as good as anybody in the country doing what they were doing. It was just a matter of time before they got discovered.

Sid was a great guy for us. It was a start-up company, when you don't even know what the hell is going to happen from one week to the next and you don't even know if your strategies are right or if you are going to raise enough money, because it was a brand-new industry and nobody really had a game plan that was proven. There's a lot of anxiety in a start-up. You have all these new employees. We went from zero to 50 employees in just a few months. Where a guy like Sid was a huge importance to us was in that he was a guy who had a great personality and could bullshit with everybody and get everybody in the right frame of mind. He was a good guy for morale, and you need guys good for morale at start-up companies. I never really knew about many of his problems or anything until later, after they were already history. I probably never knew too much about what any of my employees were up to in their private time.

In December 2004 we sold the company in its entirety to CBS. I had a three-year noncompete that didn't end until December 2007. In early 2008, I started thinking about whether I wanted to do anything else again, and I started to look at the sports sites that were out there—CBS, ESPN, Yahoo, Fox—and I just thought none of them were really innovative. They were kind of living off what they had done. And the best fantasy software, the one we created for CBS, was a nine-year-old product. It was time for a new technology. I started a company to do that and launched OPENSports. We're taking fantasy to a new level. After I started OPENSports I called Sid. Sid's been an instrumental part for us. He does videos for us every week, writes blogs. He's been a really good guy for us. There's nobody who knows any more about sports than him, and he has a way of presenting sports stuff in an entertaining way. He's a great guy.

WE NOW INTERRUPT OUR REGULARLY SCHEDULED BROADCAST
FOR A WORD FROM…

SCOTT KAPLAN, Cohost of the
Scott and BR Show on 1090 AM, San Diego

It was 1996. I was working down in Florida at a company called SportsLine.com. They hired me to start an online sports radio station. Sid's walking around like he's the mayor. His shirt is wide open, like down to his belly button, no chest at all, hair sticking out, and a big, fat smile to where you couldn't even see his eyes because they're closed. He's walking around shaking people's hands, he doesn't put his whole hand in; he grabs the fingertips, "How ya doing, how ya doing?" like he's the fucking mayor, and I'm like, "Who is this kid?" I found out pretty soon that he is a total stats geek. He's a fantasy football commissioner, and he's trying to get people online to start fantasy football teams and spend whatever it was back in the early days of online sports fantasy nonsense. He's fresh out of drug rehab, and he has this personality where he's walking around the room making everybody laugh and acting like he knows everything about everything in sports. And if he doesn't know it he'll fight you 'til the death because he has to be right, because he's from Brooklyn, and if you're from Brooklyn it means you've never been wrong about anything in your life.

I had a kid working on the air in the role of information sports geek, and I was supposed to be the comedy personality part of it. This kid wasn't working out, and I convinced the management there to let me have Sid come take that role. They didn't care. They were in an experimental mode. They didn't give a shit so they said, "Sure, go ahead." I'm the person who, unfortunately, gave Sid the crack that is radio.

We had instant chemistry. It worked out perfectly. I talked about all the nonsense I wanted to talk about, and he filled in all the gaps with the sports information and a strong sports opinion. It was a total yin-yang thing. He's a fucking out-of-control moron who has absolutely no control of himself anywhere, unless his wife's around. If his wife has a leash on him then he's fine. He's cute Sidney. If his wife is nowhere around to put the leash on him, then he's out of control, devil Sidney.

When we started out we were broadcasting on the Internet. Nobody was listening to us. Then we got syndicated by a terrestrial radio company, at the time out of Las Vegas, called Sports Fan Radio Network, which was a fledgling operation at best. They gave us freedom to do anything we wanted to do. It wasn't sports talk. It was entertainment talk with sports behind it. Sid was very much into having as much fun as we could, getting as many laughs as possible. Then when we got to New York and did a show at WNEW, he kind of changed his whole tune. He didn't want to be a laughingstock. He didn't want to be a comedian to the guys at WFAN, because his dream was always to be at WFAN. So the minute he got on the air in New York he was immediately kissing their asses.

We got to New York and we thought we were in the perfect position, the absolute money seat. We were working for Westwood One. They brought us to New York. We were with CBS Radio, and we had a home base in New York City. I told Sid, "We're not sports geeks, we're entertainers. This is show business." I built that original radio show as a complete rip-off of Howard Stern. I was Howard. He was Robin [Quivers]. I told him years and years ago, this whole talking sports, *Mike and the Mad Dog* shit is garbage. At that point I was thinking Chris Russo and Mike Francesa were two old guys already. We were young, and I felt we should be doing entertainment talk with sports in the background. Sid didn't want to do that back then. Now he wants to do it. If he would have listened to me 10 years ago, right now we would have taken over for Stern. When Stern went to satellite radio, our show—having worked for CBS, having been at WNEW, having been syndicated by Westwood One, having had a role on the Sunday NFL broadcast—was in perfect position to be in the family at CBS.

Our show at WNEW lasted less than a year. I've gone out to San Diego, I have a family of four now, I'm completely happy living out here, and life is great. I've gone on to have great success, not to sound like an arrogant asshole. Am I bitter all these years later? Of course not. I'm more upset that Sid ruined relationships. We're close again in a sort of superficial kind of way. If Sid could have controlled himself we could right now both be making a lot of money and be in a really, really big-time position in New York right now.

Sid puts on a funny show. I laugh my ass off. He's a funny guy, a good talk show host. He loves to brag about himself and make himself a much bigger star than he is. I think that's one of the funniest things ever. Talk radio for him is crack.

Howdy, Pardners

SCOTT KAPLAN

Scott Kaplan was my first partner. I worked with him on *The Drive* in Florida between 1997 and 2000 and then again in 2000 on WNEW in New York. We had a nasty, ugly breakup in 2000, as most partners usually do. It took a couple of years, but we patched things up. Scott and I had a good thing in Florida, a show that was just on Internet radio for a while before it was syndicated by Sports Fan Radio Network on a bunch of cities across America. After that, Westwood One took us on, and Joel Hollander put us on a bunch of cities across America. At the same time, Scott and I were hosting *The NFL Today* on Westwood One, the pregame show for NFL football across America. We had a good thing going.

Then we got to WNEW, and overnight, everything we had been doing wasn't really what they wanted. We sold them one bill of goods, and WNEW wanted another. It happens. Sometimes you go with a plan, and you have to change the plan. But they got pretty impatient pretty fast, and that relationship ended. Scott left and I stayed on, and I think that hurt us. He probably felt that since we came there together, we should have fought for each other to keep our thing going, or we should have left together. I think it bothered him that I stuck around and did mornings at WNEW. At the end, he felt I wasn't loyal to him. Six months into it he was gone. There has been very little communication for a couple of years between Scott and me.

We had our issues in the end. There was a lot of ego, some personal stuff that got in the way and a clear-cut difference in philosophy. The bottom line? Scott and I were good together, but he wasn't good enough to be a big-time host in New York. And I had set my sights on the FAN.

CRAIG CARTON

After my split from Kaplan at WNEW, I went through a bunch of different partners. I had John Riggins in there for a week, and I had Jay Glazer in there for a week. My next full-time partner was Craig Carton in 2000. I had worked with Craig prior to WNEW at SportsLine. Scott and I had the marquee show at SportsLine, and Carton was kind of the next best thing there. So when I got to WNEW and I was looking for a cohost, we tried out a bunch of different people. Eventually Jeremy Coleman, who was the program director, got Craig Carton's résumé on his desk.

I told him I'd worked with Carton down in Florida and suggested that we give him a shot. Energetic and conversational was his shtick. He had gotten into trouble in Philadelphia for the Eric Lindros story and all that nonsense. The Flyers said Lindros was hurt, and Craig said, "No, he was just out drinking last night." The Flyers ended up suing the station, and it ended up a big mess. I was aware of all that, but as far as I was concerned, it didn't matter. I thought he was pretty good, there was a comfort factor there, so I thought we should bring him in.

Early on, it was fine. We got along great. We were hanging out off the air, playing ball together. Eventually, we just had two totally different philosophies. Craig brought a lot of the shtick he had over at WIP in Philadelphia, like during the NCAA basketball tournament let's not talk basketball, but let's take Italian dishes and make our own bracket for the top 64. Veal parmigiana vs. fettuccine alfredo. I wasn't a big fan of that. At one point he actually had a snake eat a rabbit live in the studio. On the radio! He described the whole thing. I actually walked out of the studio that day.

I'll admit I was a little frustrated. When Craig got there, I was still hosting the show. There was a host chair in front of the computer, and then there were chairs around the table for the cohosts. I was in that host chair, but it didn't take long for Craig to move in. At the time, I had not hosted anything else on my own. I had been Scott's cohost for years. He was the guy who took us in and out of breaks. I had no hosting experience and Craig did. If they would have hired just one guy to host day one I think they would have given it to Craig over me in a heartbeat. But the fact was that it was already my show. I had been there for six months, and he was coming in and saying, "I'll do anything you want to make this work," and a week later he's sitting in the host chair. We did whatever he wanted to do because he had success with it in a different market. I probably got pissed off and resentful early on. He came there to work with me, but it quickly became his show.

The producers wanted it to be an ensemble cast, so they brought in a third member for the show, a guy by the name of Blaine Ensley. Stupid fights would happen. I always liked Blaine. He was a real nice guy, but Blaine was in over his head. He wasn't a sports guy—he was doing pukey afternoon WPLJ radio, prank phone calls and that type of thing—and all of a sudden he became a sports talk show host. I don't think so.

Blaine was not a sports guy, and the name of the show was *The Sports Guys*. It was ridiculous. Back then, my philosophy was different. Now, I encourage talking more of the non-sports stuff. In fact I encourage it. But in 2000 I didn't have the experience—I hadn't worked at FAN yet, hadn't worked for Don Imus yet. I was still new in the game and I was still trying to be a sports guy. Doing mornings in New York City, I knew I had to be credible, knew I had to be that sports guy. That was my comfort zone. And to a certain extent I was right, because in the end Mark Chernoff and WFAN hired me based upon my work at WNEW. If I had been clowning around like Craig Carton and Blaine, I never would have gotten the job. I wasn't playing all the reindeer games, if you will. I'd walk out of the studio, and Craig and Blaine would be doing something silly and the program director would ask me what I was doing. I would say, "I'm not doing this shit. This is fucking nonsense." It was child's play, sophomoric bullshit.

I had a one-year deal, and the second year was a station option. I came on in April 2000. In April 2001 I went down to Florida, like I do every year, for Passover. I was there for four or five days, and I'm ready to come back even though I'm fighting with Craig Carton and having a miserable time of it and everybody knew it. I was starting to get a little bit of a following, so I was certain that I was coming back for year two, that they're going to pick up the option.

I don't know why, but I checked my messages at home on my way to the airport. There was a message from Jeremy Coleman, my program director: "Do me a favor, Sid. Before you get back from Florida give me a buzz." It seemed innocent. So I called him:

"Hey Jeremy, what's up? I had a great trip."

"Did you have a really good trip? Do you love it there?"

"Yeah, it's a nice place to visit."

"Why don't you stay?"

"Stay? I'm coming home. I'm on the air tomorrow."

And he says, "Nah, you're not on the air tomorrow."

At that point I really was shocked. Carton stayed and I left. Unbelievable. Carton stuck around for a while with Blaine Ensley, and eventually Scott Ferrall took over for them both. Then again, I won, because I went to the FAN. We used have these screaming fights where Carton would say, "You want to go to FAN. You don't want to be here." Of course I wanted to go to the FAN! Those few months with Craig turned out to be a disaster. We had issues along the way that got in the way, probably some resentment and jealousies on both sides. It did not end well.

Years and years later, Craig was on a show in New Jersey on 101.5 called *The Jersey Guys*. That show had a lot of success, and that's how Craig got the job at WFAN. Chernoff lives in Livingston, New Jersey, and he heard that show and liked it and Craig.

I have relatives that live in central Jersey, and every time I got into trouble with Imus, went to rehab, or whatever, they would come back to me and say, "That guy Craig is killing you today." There was obviously some resentment over the years. We have since buried the hatchet. I don't think we're ever going to end up being the best of friends, but at least now there's no fights. Off the air he's really charming, quite frankly. For a good eight years we maintained this animosity for each other. It all ended in October 2008 with a 10-minute cell phone conversation.

Craig's done a real good job with the WFAN morning show. he's brought a lot of attention to mornings, not just by doing a local TV spot of walking across the Brooklyn Bridge in a Speedo. He and Boomer Esiason have a good chemistry. With all the money and publicity that went to Imus we never sniffed number one in the ratings. He's a talented kid.

Jody McDonald

Jody McDonald was my next partner for middays on WFAN, on *The Mac and Sid Show*. Jody is a really good guy, prepared, smart, and just a nice guy. He is truly one of the nicest guys in the business. For the most part we had a really, really good rapport and a good time. We worked together from 2001 to 2004.

A lot of the time, if something happened on *Imus* it came up every now and then on the midday show. There were a lot of times Jody was pretty uncomfortable with that. Jody became a sort of father figure. He wasn't my contemporary; he is 10 years older than me. I was getting into trouble or something was leaking over from the *Imus* show; we'd have a father-son dynamic. Ninety-nine percent of the time it was fine. We're both pretty big sports fans, and he was really easy to work with. The only time there was even a little bit of an issue was with that type of thing, when I started to go into stuff that wasn't centered around the world of sports or was a little over the line.

JOE BENIGNO

Joe Benigno took over for Jody, and that was great. Did Joe love everything I talked about? Probably not. But we're close friends, so there was never an issue. He never would walk out upset or grumpy like every other cohost I had—even Jody or Scott. You hear the whispering between that person and the producer, "I don't want to talk about this or that today." But even when Joe didn't want to hop on the bus with me, that never happened. It was just easy, every day. Joe's a good soldier. He knew the deal, that along with the *Imus* thing there was going to be some crazy stuff that went on, and he didn't mind it.

People out there paint Joe as this "Mr. Jets Fan, Mr. Mets fan," as if that's where it begins and ends. It's not true. There are a lot of other things he likes as well. The guy's a big music fan; he could talk music 24 hours a day. He has other interests outside the world of sports. I think Joe is one of those guys who appreciates where he is. He's there deservedly so, by the way, because no one made it easy for him. The guy won a fucking contest, and he had to do all those overnights to get where he is today. He genuinely appreciates it, and he treats it that way.

There was nothing like a Monday morning after a Jets loss, nothing like it. The Giants might have lost as well, and I was upset about the Giants, but I probably was more upset about something that happened at home or something that happened in the world. Look, the one thing New Yorkers always say about me—I get a million messages, even now, and I'm out of New York for more than four years—is the passion. People thought about FAN in terms of the passion. They thought about Benigno, about me, about Chris Russo. They weren't thinking about Mike Francesa or Chris Carlin or Adam Schein.

There was nothing like that Monday morning rant by Benigno after a Jets loss. A lot of Mondays I would come in and just say, "Go, just go." He would ask me, "Yo, bro, you want to talk about the Giants?" *No, just go.* We're both Mets fans, so when he had a Mets rant I jumped in here and there, but his rants are simply the best. They're not scripted, he's not trying to be funny or trying to get a rise out of people—that's just how he feels. The guy takes it to heart like no one I've ever met, which is great, especially at FAN, which really needs that.

To this day, we're best friends. I love him to death, but we're two totally different animals. Benigno is the type of guy who can do 10:00 AM to 1:00 PM the rest of his life. He's making a nice living and has a nice little house in New Jersey and he's happy. That's not me. I have to be doing 90,000 things at once. Benigno doesn't even know how to use a computer. He doesn't have an e-mail address, and I'm on Facebook and Twitter for four hours a night. We're totally different animals. I thought we had a great show together. He wasn't upset at the FAN about the same things as me. I think he'll be happy there for the rest of his life. There's nothing wrong with that—it's a great gig. But me, I was always felt like, *Yeah, it's kind of cool, but I want more.*

Joe is a guy who became a star and he's got no ego. That's almost impossible in this business today. Even the young kids who are weekend hacks walk around with an ego. Not Joe. He's great at what he does; that's enough for him. I've made some great friends in this business and he is right there at the top of the list. All the love, bro!

IAN EAGLE

I did a lot of stuff with Ian Eagle. Over the summer we filled in for Mike and the Mad Dog, and that was a great show. In terms of what FAN always wants, that Mike and Chris dynamic, Joe and I are both kind of hotheads and both kind of wild, so that didn't fit that mold. Ian and I were closer, since Ian is kind of laid back and very cerebral. He has the experience, he knows everybody, worked everywhere. Those qualities are like Mike. And then you have me, yelling and screaming. I would even take on more of that "wild man" role with Ian than I would with other partners because I knew it would appease Mark Chernoff and those guys. I wanted them to think, *Wow, that's the next* Mike and the Mad Dog. We had great shows, funny and informative, and we have a great relationship to this day. I think he's brilliant and wickedly funny.

Scott Ferrall

I had one memorable show with Scott Ferrall. Actually, the show for which he was fired from the FAN was the one he did with me. He was on for a little while, doing fill-ins and weekend shit. Chernoff liked him. He's crazy. I love Scott; he's great. Our careers are similar in the respect that I think we've been fired more than anybody else. Maybe Howard Stern and Imus have been fired more times, but in sports, Ferrall and I have similar pedigrees.

We were doing a show on a Saturday night, and it was early on in my FAN career. I didn't do a lot of stuff on the weekends outside of the Giants games. That night, Felix Trinidad was fighting Bernard Hopkins at Madison Square Garden. Both Ferrall and I are huge boxing fans, and we both liked to bet on sports back then. It was a huge college football day, so it was perfect. We were going to do a Saturday night show, talk about all the college football action from the afternoon on a station on which nobody really talks about college football. And then we were going to talk about the fight. We actually went together in a limo to the fight.

About midway through the show we got a call from Doris from Rego Park. She was on the show with me and Jody Mac all the time—she had been a favorite caller on the FAN for years, I loved her, and she loved me. So she called up and started that coughing routine. She was sick. I think she had throat cancer or something. She's dead now, God rest her soul. So Ferrall has no idea who she is, no idea what she meant to the station, and he makes a comment. It was in poor taste, but he couldn't have known she was really ill.

One thing about WFAN is they treat some of their callers like children, like their own kids. We kind of make fun of them in the newsroom, the chronic callers, and other listeners may make fun of them. But the powers that be understand they're the lifeline of the station. So when Doris from Rego Park calls every single day, you may find it annoying and the listeners may find it annoying, but that's what makes FAN what it is.

So she calls up this Saturday night and starts, "The Mets today Sidney...cough, cough, cough...the Mets today...cough cough, cough, cough, cough." And Ferrall is saying, "C'mon Doris, you can get that out. C'mon, get it out, Doris." And on the other end, the poor lady is dying of throat cancer. And he kept saying that every time she would choke—and she would choke 30 times a minute! Here it is like 10:00 on a Saturday night, and we're thinking no one's listening anyway. This guy has no idea who the fuck Doris from Rego Park is, and I'm thinking that we have to break when the phone rings in the control room. It's Chernoff. Busted.

Scott and I were so flammable that even though Chernoff was really excited about the idea and thought it could be a great show, he was nervous about us—which is why he was listening at home, at 10:00 PM on a Saturday. Program directors never listen on the weekends. Ever. Chernoff went berserk on Scott for making fun of Doris. I think it was two days later that they whacked him.

O.J. McDUFFIE

When I first started in the business in Miami, I had a bunch of different producers. My producer for the longest time was Allyson Turner. I happened to have contact with her and this guy John Weiner, nicknamed "Stugotz." He was the producer of *The Hank Goldberg Show* down in Miami for many years. I got to know him when I was down in Miami between 1997 and 2000. When I went the FAN, Weiner and Allison Turner were at a station down here, a start-up sports station, 790 The Ticket.

Weiner was a huge fan of mine, and his father and mother still lived up in New York. He listened to me on the FAN every single day. He was starting up this station, and offered me a bunch of money. So when I did lose my job I kind of knew I had that in the bag. The good news was, it wasn't run by a major company like CBS. The ticket was owned by a local kid named Joel Feinberg, a real nice, rich Jewish kid whose father made millions and millions of dollars. Joel bought the station and he ran it. There was no public group behind it, so I didn't have to go through a board of directors to get hired. Even though after I was fired I lost my leverage and I couldn't command the big salary that I once could, I knew that eventually they were going to hire me. They knew what I could do on the air. I just had to convince this one kid.

I went down to Florida in September 2005, and I finally got on the air in November. Initially when I was hired, they were very nervous because I was very New York. So when I first started working, my partner, who was already on the air, was former Dolphins standout O.J. McDuffie. *Great.* Most Dolphins fans will tell you that he's probably the fourth-best receiver they ever had. Paul Warfield's a Hall of Famer, then you have Mark Duper and Mark Clayton with Dan Marino. Then there's O.J. He's beloved in Miami, but he had a toe injury that forced him to leave the game quite young.

I was out of work for two months. It was tremendously embarrassing, and I took a huge cut in pay. I had been making six figures, and my first job at 790 was less—way less. But it got me on the air, which is what I had to do, and it got me back in the game. Obviously O.J. had some resentment because he saw me come into town, this fast-talking, loudmouth New Yorker. He's a Dolphin guy, so he hates New Yorkers. Right away they assume I'm a Jets fan, which I'm not. I'm a Giants fan. Lucky break. So we both hated the Jets, one thing we had in common.

We got off to a bit of a rough start. In fact, one month into working together, the Dolphins had played Buffalo. They were getting killed, but Sage Rosenfels staged this ridiculous, improbable comeback, and the Dolphins got three TDs in the fourth quarter to beat the Buffalo Bills. On the same Sunday, Tiki Barber had a monster game in a Giants win. I went into work the following Monday. I had been on the air in Miami for only about one month. I had made it very, very clear from day one that I had no problem with them, I was working with one of greatest players of all time, but under no circumstances was I a Dolphins fan. I am a Giants fan. So I went on the air and started with Tiki and the Giants. By the time I got to the Dolphins and the Bills, instead of me giving Miami heaps credit for this amazing comeback, I got on the Buffalo coach, Mike Mularkey, because he had J.P. Losman throw the ball all over the field, throwing touchdowns, and they literally went into the run-out-the-clock offense in the second quarter.

This started a huge fight in the studio, the worst I've ever had on the air. Nasty. And I walked out and left, which I've almost never done. I've had bad fights on the air—with Imus, Jody Mac. I got up, said, "Fuck you," and I left. It was bad. I was back on the air for a month, and I'm only three months removed from this New York fiasco. I got phone calls from guys up in New York, *What the fuck happened? What did you do? Oh, God, Sid fucking lost it again* and *Maybe Sid's high. Who the fuck knows?*

My boss called me that afternoon and said, "You can't walk off the air in the middle of the show."

I said, "Fuck you. I didn't work six years doing middays up in New York at FAN, the greatest station in the history of this medium, and work with Imus and all these great guys to come down to this shit hole, this fucking rotten sports town with a guy that's never been on the air before to be told how to do a fucking radio show." It got nasty. O.J. was saying that he'd kick my ass.

So Weiner was the guy in charge at the time, and he asked me to come back. I was like, *I'm not coming back. Fuck you guys.* And the next day neither one of us came to work. And then the next day, for what it's worth, I called O.J. and we talked. I knew that it was going to blow over. We moved on. And for that one day, the station enjoyed it because it got publicity all over the place—all over Florida. It even made the papers up in New York. After that one day I called O.J. and we kind of patched things up and we were back on the air together the next day. By the way, to this day, we're still very good friends. O.J. left the station about 18 months into our partnership. He was unhappy with the way the station was being run—and he didn't need the money, quite frankly. I worked alone after that.

Even after he left, Juice and I stayed in touch. He's got a big heart—and he's one of the most charitable athletes I've ever met. His Catch 81 Foundation is constantly raising money for great causes in Miami. I'm proud to say that we're friends

WE NOW INTERRUPT OUR REGULARLY SCHEDULED BROADCAST FOR A WORD FROM…

CRAIG CARTON, Cohost,
The Boomer and Carton Show on WFAN

We met in the late summer, early fall of 1997. At the time I was working at WIP radio in Philly and had been hired by a guy named Ross Levinson to go down to Florida to work for this upstart company, SportsLine. They were in the process of syndicating radio shows. They needed someone who had actually been on the radio and been successful on the radio. Sid was doing a show, which at the time was only on the Internet, with a fellow by the name of Scott Kaplan.

Before I ever heard him on the radio I thought he was this crazy, kind of loud, obnoxious guy from New York, which reminded me a lot of home. We got along well from day one, before I learned about all his vices and issues. We started playing basketball on a semiregular basis the first couple of weeks I was out there.

He's always said he was instrumental in getting me to WNEW. The way it played out, Scott Kaplan got fired in early 2000. I had just come back to the East Coast from Denver. My wife was pregnant with our first child, and I had just come back to WIP. I sent my stuff into Jeremy Coleman, who at the time was the program director at WNEW. Sid has told the story, and I have no reason to doubt it, that when they were looking for Scott's replacement, and they brought basically every guy with a pulse through that door, that Sid saw my package on the program director's desk and said something to the effect of, "I've worked with Craig. He's a good guy. Maybe give him a look." Beyond that I'm not sure what he did or didn't do.

When I came in at WNEW it was me, Sid, a comedian by the name of Eddie Ifft, and two or three other rotating people. On Monday and Friday, Billy Taylor, the football player, would be a part of our show. John Riggins came by on a regular basis. We were nicknamed "Menudo" by Opie and Anthony because you never knew who was hosting the show from one day to the next. It was always someone different in there. That whole thing was a clusterfuck.

When Sid and I did the show, we were coming at it from two different places, purely from what we wanted to do on the radio. I was brought in because I did more of a "guy talk" show, which wasn't straightforward *sports, sports, sports,* and Sid was coming at it wanting to do straight sports. It's amazing—he wound up getting into a lot of trouble at the FAN later in life for *not* doing straight sports. We battled a few times over my desire to make it a little less sports-oriented and his desire to make it much more sports-oriented. He made no secret of the fact that his dream job was not there; it was WFAN and he thought he had the chops to get there, which clearly he did.

I always resented a lot of his off-air things. We always got along, but when you look at it professionally, the goal for anyone in what we do for a living is to get to New York, especially if you are a New Yorker, as I am and as he was. The goal—whether it's the FAN or WNEW, I don't care where you go—is to get to New York and do mornings. I always resented the fact his off-radio drama really put a dent in our ability to be successful as a team. Now, we weren't successful for myriad reasons. I resented him having all this other shit going on that made it so he couldn't focus on what we were trying to accomplish, whether we agreed on a philosophy or not.

He was able to pull it together for the most part. But his problems became a daily grind for him. Almost every commercial break you're banging your head against the wall because you're not sure if when he walks out the door someone might be there to punch him in the face. Clearly he was doing things after a certain hour when I was probably sleeping that got him into trouble and put him in a bad spot, but he showed up for work every day. I've always said that he's wonderfully talented. He's just one of those conflicted guys who, at least up to that point, couldn't get his personal shit worked out. And unfortunately he's paid for that in a large way with his career.

There's no denying the fact he's a very talented guy in an industry where I just don't think there are that many talented, standout guys. The problem is that he never allowed his talent to drive his life; he's allowed his demons to drive his life, and that got in the way of his talent. That's taking chances on the air, saying things on the air, that's not maturing on the air. Listen, I've said things and gotten in trouble, but at some point you grow up. He never grew up in that regard, up to that point.

My controversies were about me saying something, having an opinion about something on the air and that opinion being delicate to this person or that person. Unfortunately, Sid went from being a great personality to almost a caricature of a great personality, and it's a fine line. We all fight it. He became that after he started working with Imus. I've never met Don Imus before but my guess is Sid was so eager to please him and so eager to deliver what he thought Imus wanted that he kind of lost sight of what he should be doing for himself. I'm playing schoolyard shrink here, but that's my guess.

I got a call at 9:00 PM from a producer at WNEW saying, "You're going to be by yourself tomorrow morning. Sid got fired," and that's how I found out. My reaction wasn't "Thank God." I was shocked. I wasn't expecting it. I knew there were issues there, some performance issues because of his other stuff, but I didn't cry over it either.

It did not end well with us at WNEW. He owed me money at the time, and I thought he was partly responsible for our show not succeeding. Immediately after that, I kind of let the world know that, and he responded when he was hired finally down in Florida that he didn't think I was the nicest guy in the world. That little feud, kind of a third-person feud because we weren't talking to each other at the time, kind of lasted almost like a Cold War until the summer of 2008. He thought he was going to get hired back in New York and wanted to make amends with me because at that point I was doing mornings at FAN and, knock on wood, Boomer and I were successful. He thought that if he did get the job there—and I don't know how close he was—it wouldn't make sense for anybody for him to come in and have a feud with a guy who was on the air already. I don't know that we're going out to dinner any time soon. We're not. I understand why he called to reconcile. It was a strategic move, for sure. I have a great job, I have a wife and three kids there are other things on my radar much more important than whether I'm getting along with Sid, or anyone else, really. I thought he manned up and did the right thing. Maybe it took him too long, but he made the phone call he had to make and we're good.

He had it all. What they always say about Sid—he has more lives than a cat. The thing about Sid is that he can charm your pants off. He's very charming when he wants to be and knows how to play that game. The fact is he got fired at WNEW. That he had all the issues he had and still landed at the FAN and was given all those chances at the FAN to make good is really remarkable, and it says a lot about his talent.

We all grew up in New York listening to Howard Stern. Certainly none of us do what Howard does, but there are parts of Howard we all kind of took into our shtick and our act because they're successful. When you're a kid growing up in New York and there's this great personality, Howard Stern, and you go into radio yourself, how can it not rub off on you a little bit? It certainly did for me, and I would imagine Sid says it did for him, too. I never got Imus. My dad was an Imus guy, but I never understood why people fawned over Imus. I never thought he was funny; I never understood what the big deal was. To guys our age, Howard Stern is the best of all time. In my career people say, "You're the Howard Stern of sports," and they think that's a put-down. That's a great compliment to me. It would be to Sid, too.

Sid idolized Chris Russo. That was his guy. When we were at WNEW, Sid's screen-saver was a picture of Chris Russo. That's the guy he wanted to be. He idolized Chris, not Mike Francesa. I always felt Sid knew as much as Mike as far as, "I can pull a stat out of my ass from the last 40 years." That's an ability I don't have the way those guys have it. Sid has it the way Mike does, but Sid wants to be Russo, not Francesa. I know he's much closer to Mike, which is an amazing dynamic. Mike has an affinity for Sid still. Look, I don't know Mike that well, I don't get along with Mike that well, but it is interesting to me he has an affinity for Sid and that he kind of embraces Sid is fascinating. Don't forget, Mike idolizes Imus, and the fact Imus kind of vouches for Sid, maybe that changed Mike's opinion. Everything Sid is, to me, is everything that

Mike hates. So the fact Mike has a soft spot in his heart for Sid makes me interested in that dynamic. It's a little circus we have going on here. It's just fascinating to me. When the ratings came out in summer of 2009, Boomer and I were the highest-rated morning show in the history of the FAN. Mike will never have that place for me in his heart that he has for Sid. Mike will never think of me, though I couldn't care less, the way he thinks of Sid.

You have guys like Mushnick of the *Post* and Raissman of the *Daily News*, the guys that get paid to be critical, and they lump a lot of us in together. If you've ever gotten into any kind of trouble in your career, and it doesn't matter what the trouble was, you're now a trouble maker or "shock jock." My issues and Sid's issues are very different, but yet we do get lumped in together. Luckily, I'm too old to care about what those guys write.

I think Sid and I would do a great show together. I do. I don't know who would be the alpha male in that show, but I think we would at this point in our lives do a very good show together.

One Sid story: we were both working at WNEW, and the Giants were in the Super Bowl against the Ravens after the 2000 season. We flew down to Tampa for the Super Bowl, and he and I were roommates together for the three, four days. We didn't have tickets to the game. So we did all our shows for the Super Bowl, and then Sid and I—we were with Blaine Ensley at the time—were sitting in a shitty Motel 6, with a little sports bar area. The three of us and Fred Smerlas of the Buffalo Bills, who apparently doesn't have a ticket to the game either, were watching the game. We must have ordered tons and tons of beer and several hundred chicken wings. It was probably a $300 bar tab because we were drinking pretty heavily. Sid has $10,000 on the New York Giants, and it's evident by halftime that he ain't gonna win that bet because the Giants are getting blown out. So the tab comes, and the question is, who's gonna pay the tab? Fred Smerlas, the All-Pro football player from back in the day? Me? Or the guy that just lost $10,000 on the Giants? So the tab comes, and Sid says to the waitress, "Put it on my room." And that's Sid Rosenberg.

If Anyone Asks, I'd Rather Be Alone

I'd much rather be a one-man act. Now does that mean I wouldn't work with somebody again? Of course not. Of course I would, but hope it's the right guy. Listen, I've got Attention Deficit Disorder; there's no question in my mind. My mind moves very, very quickly. I believe that my mind moves faster than 99.9 percent of the people in this population. I'm just not capable of staying with one topic for too long—you know what I'm saying?

I like the fact that when I'm doing a solo show I can be talking about the Giants and mid-sentence transition to something else and not worry that the person I'm sitting with might say, "Wait a second. We were just talking about the Giants. Hold on. What are you talking about?" Especially because I talk about so many other things outside of sports. A lot of guys don't like to talk politics or aren't familiar with what's going on with politics. I don't feel like explaining after the show to anyone why I thought X topic was the right thing to discuss. It's just easier to be alone. Look, you go down in flames, you go down in flames. That's fine.

I wouldn't mind having like a sidekick, somebody that could kind of chime in every now and then, but I'm not looking to go 50-50. Very few guys are capable of going four to five hours by themselves. Most guys like to have somebody next to them that they can bounce stuff off or who can save the day if you have a bad voice that day. If you're tired that day, it's good to have somebody next to you who can help out. But anybody with an ego who has had some success in this business as a host, 99 percent of the guys want to have a sidekick type of guy but would still want to be The Guy. Howard Stern is still The Guy. I don't care how much Robin talks, I don't care how much Artie talks or Jackie or Fred, Howard is still The Guy. I don't care how much Charles talks or Bernard talks or Rob talks or Lou talks, Imus is still The Guy and at the end of the day, Imus is going to be the one who starts the conversation, and he's gonna end the conversation. If he likes what you're talking about he may participate. If he doesn't he may say, "Fuck this, it's over." I don't know anybody who doesn't want that.

You Have to Be Damn Good to Be Fired So Many Times

Every time I got fired from *Imus* I thought, *You know what? He's still a legend. He's a pioneer in the business. Before there was a Howard Stern, there was a Don Imus, and when it's all said and done, even though I fucked up a couple of times, I can tell my kids I worked with Imus.*

I got really only fired twice. I was fired for the comment about Venus and Serena Williams in June 2001 and for what I said about Kylie Minogue in May 2005. I was *almost* suspended after the in 2003 Super Bowl in San Diego, and I was suspended for four days for not showing up after the Republican National Convention.

It's June of 2001, and Bud Collins is on the phone from France, it was the French Open, and we started talking about Venus and Serena Williams. Bo Dietl was in the studio along with me and Imus. I said, "One time a friend, he says to me, 'Listen, one of these days you're gonna see Venus and Serena Williams in *Playboy*.' And I said, 'You've got a better shot at *National Geographic*.'" Imus was laughing. Everybody was laughing. The funny thing is, I had no idea at the time I had done or said anything that was all that bad. They were kind of laughing and feigning that "Oh my God" posture, but it didn't seem horrible at the time. The show ended like any other.

But as the day progressed, it got worse and worse. By the time I left the station a couple of hours later, Mark Chernoff had been telling me, "We got another call from this paper, from that paper.... This is getting worse. I would stick by the phone if I were you." I'll never forget—my wife had gone on vacation to Florida that day to visit her grandmother. I was living in Riverdale in the Bronx. I got a call every couple of hours from Chernoff, and eventually I talked to him at 7:00 that night. He said, "Look, this thing is getting bad—the *Post,* the *News,* the *Times,* this magazine, that magazine." He said, "At the very least you're suspended." I'm not sure if I got fired that day or not. I think they wanted to see how bad it would be the next day.

I went to bed that night, alone in the Bronx, and the phone rang at 5:00 AM It was Danielle, and she was hysterical. She had gotten up early to go work out in the gym down in Florida and went to buy the paper just in case, because she knew what was going on. She looked at the whole sports section, and there was nothing mentioned about me. She breathed a sigh of relief. *Okay, great, we dodged a bullet. No big deal. Imus is kind of controversial. The show is kind of crazy. Maybe it wasn't as big as we thought it was going to be.* Then she goes to the front of the paper, and they had a huge picture of me and Venus on page three of the *New York Post.* I can hear her voice as clear as a bell. "I can't believe this," she said. "You're 33 years old and you're done. It's over." And I was thinking, *Holy shit, I am done.*

Throughout the day I listened to other radio shows. Howard Stern was sticking up for me. Sean Hannity was sticking up for me. All these guys talking about the First Amendment are sticking up for me, saying I shouldn't be fired, especially by a guy like Imus. Here I was, in the radio business for a couple of years and I had never really had any publicity. Down in Florida, on SportsLine and Westwood One nobody had any idea who the fuck I was. Nothing I ever did really got any publicity. And then I said this one thing about Serena and

Venus on the *Imus* show, and I'm everywhere. I had people calling my house, Opie and Anthony asked me to come on and talk about it. I put on the radio, and Rush Limbaugh was talking about it. It was everywhere.

At that point I figured I was fired, even with the groundswell of support that was going on for me throughout the day. No one supported my comments. They all thought it was pretty fucked up, but they said, "Hey, it's the First Amendment. The kid didn't know. It's his first offense." Then the phone call eventually came to my house. It was from Kara Dugan, Imus' secretary.

"I-Man wants to talk to you," she said, and she put him through. This is my house in Riverdale, and it's Imus on the other end of the phone. I barely know him at this point. I had met him like four or five times, and now he's calling my fucking apartment? He says, "Listen, you fucked up. You have to write a letter of apology to the two girls and the father. You'll read the letter on the air. Be sincere about it. I've made my mistakes. We'll bring you back and see you next Tuesday." Click.

And just like that, I was back.

My next problem had nothing to do with Imus. I went out to the Super Bowl in San Diego in January 2003, the year the Buccaneers played the Raiders. I went out there with my buddy, Vin. Chernoff really didn't want me to go, and I convinced him, "C'mon, I'm paying my own way. You're not even paying for me." I was hosting a party out there for TrimSpa. They were paying for everything—the hotel, the flights, all that plus a nice little bonus on top. I was actually one of the spokespeople for TrimSpa (and after I left, Anna Nicole Smith became their spokesperson). They were having this huge party out at the Super Bowl, and they invited me to come out there.

Chernoff protested, "You're not even doing anything for us."

So I said, "Here's what I'll do for you. I'll do a show live from the Super Bowl, Saturday late afternoon, for our listeners back in New York. I'll be out there live on radio row, giving them a taste of the Super Bowl." I figured that would make Chernoff happy and take the pressure off me.

Friday night was the party. They had this big red carpet. It was me, Pat O'Brien (who at the time was with *Access Hollywood*), Carmen Electra, and Nicole Eggert, the young and beautiful blonde from *Charles in Charge* who went on to *Baywatch* for many years. She had quite a following. We have a blast that night. It was a long party, obviously. The party went late Friday into Saturday, and I was supposed to be on the air that next day. I called Chris Carlin—he had gone to San Diego to cover that Super Bowl for the FAN—and I told him, "Listen, bro, I can't make it." He was floored. "What do you mean you can't make it? You've got to be on the air in a couple of hours." I'm like, "Bro, *I CAN'T FUCKING MAKE IT.*"

Then I had a conversation with Mike Francesa. I said, "Listen, Carlin is busting my fucking balls, that fat bastard. Do me a favor, Mike." Mike could tell I was a fucking mess. He told me to get some sleep and not worry about it, that he'd take care of it. So that's exactly what I did. When I got back, I wasn't suspended or fired, but they did give me a letter pretty much saying if you ever do something like that again that it'd turn out ugly for me.

In September 2004 my cousin Norm Coleman was in town. He was running for senate in Minnesota, an election which he won in tragic fashion because Paul Wellstone and his whole family were killed in a plane crash. He was in town to go to the Republican National Convention, which they held in Madison Square Garden, and all the big shots were here. Chernoff and everybody were aware I was taking my cousin out that night. I ended up taking him to John McCain's party, which was at Cipriani in the city. I took him to Saxby Chambliss' party. There were a lot of politicians throwing parties that night, and my cousin lives in Minnesota. He wasn't familiar with the city, and he knew I was and knew I knew a lot of these guys through Imus. He'll never forget the reaction I got from John and Cindy McCain that night, because I'd been on with John so many times on the *Imus* show. I took my cousin to a bunch of parties that night.

I had been warned that afternoon by Chernoff, "Make sure you're here tomorrow, Sid." I told him, "I'll be there, don't worry." Of course I didn't make it in. I was out partying all night. I was suspended then and nearly fired. Imus would always feign disgust and anger, but of course you're talking about a guy who did coke and drank his whole fucking life until he got sober at close to 50 years old. There I was in my thirties, working a high-profile job in New York, out on the town. I think Imus understood it. He didn't accept it, he didn't condone it, and he wasn't okay with it—that's why I got suspended—but he understood it. That's what was kind of cool about Imus. It would be kind of hypocritical for Imus to say "You're fired because you're out on the town drinking and drugging and missed work" when it happened to Don 1,000 times. They took action, and they couldn't allow it. It wasn't like Howard Stern does with Artie Lange, when Lange shows up in the studio after a full night of drinking and doing heroin and nobody gives a shit. Don wasn't going to have that. So they suspended me for a couple of days.

In May 2005 I'm on the *Imus* show, and Bernard McGuirk and I are talking about Kylie Minogue, the very famous Australian singer who at the time was just diagnosed with breast cancer. Bernie's going back and forth about how pretty she is and I say, "She won't look so pretty when she's bald with one tit," which was horrible. I've often been asked if I regret some of the things I've said on the air. Absolutely I do, and this one is one, for sure.

I left and nothing horrible happened. I had done the show with Joe Benigno. We were doing the show from Shea Stadium that day: the Mets were playing the Reds. All of a sudden you start to get the New York City message board bings. I'm on the field interviewing Sean Casey, the Reds' first baseman, and they're in my ear from the booth upstairs, saying, "Listen, Sid, you have to go back to the station." I knew it right away. *Here we go again, another fucking disaster.* I went back to the station, and they suspended me initially. But then after a couple of days they took me off the *Imus* show for good. They kept me at the station and I continued to work with Benigno doing middays, but at that point I was off the *Imus* show for good.

I understood why Don fired me. You can't be doing that stuff on his show especially, with the pressure and scrutiny he was under. He did bring me back, and after that it was one faux pas, one fuck-up after another. I often say that Don and I are kind of like George Steinbrenner and Billy Martin: he keeps firing me, and then all of a sudden you turn on Imus' show six months later and, somehow or another, Sid Rosenberg magically appears.

I still had the midday show on WFAN with Joe, I still was hosting the New York Giants' pregame show. Then night before the 2005 season opener against the Cardinals I was going to Atlantic City. I was working at the time with *FHM* magazine, and they were having this huge fantasy football party in Atlantic City. There were hundreds and hundreds of people there, and they were going to have the fantasy football draft on Saturday afternoon and then a private party that night. I was scheduled to appear as one of the celebrities. The host was Leeann Tweeden, a personality on *The Best Damn Sports Show.* She also did a NASCAR show. She is a knockout, gorgeous. So I head to Atlantic City with my agent, Mark Lepselter, early on Saturday morning. I had to be back Sunday early afternoon because the Giants were scheduled to play the late game and I'm the pregame show host. People there were like, *Not a good idea.*

The *FHM* party was over that Saturday night. My agent and everybody else went back to their hotel rooms because they knew we were leaving early the next morning to go back to New Jersey for the game. I met one of those guys on the boardwalk who ride the little buggy things, kind of like a boardwalk taxi service. I'd had a couple of drinks at the *FHM* party, so I was ready to rock and roll. I was in that little buggy thing for two or three minutes, and I was struggling. *I'm a little fucked up here, but I have to be at the Giants thing tomorrow. I've been warned by everybody, if I fuck up here it's over. Then again, it's only 2:00 AM and I'm in Atlantic City. We're not leaving until 9:00 in the morning. If I get to bed by 4:00 AM, I can make it. Or do I just do the right thing and go back to my hotel room and just go to bed before I really fuck things up?*

Like most of the time when you're fucked up, the devil on my shoulder spoke louder. For the two or three minutes on that little buggy ride, the angel and the devil argued, but eventually the devil won out. The guy asked me, "You going back to your hotel room?" And I said, "Yeah, but it's kind of early. What do you do around this town?" He mentioned a club in one of the hotels, and next thing you know we got to talking about where to party. This guy actually hooked me up with the drugs that night that kept me up until literally 9:00 the next morning. I got paid for the appearance, got paid on the spot, which was bad. They actually paid me cash that night, so I had $1,000 to play around with. And of course I spent it on drugs.

Mark Lepselter was criticized by Chernoff, he was criticized by my family, and to be honest some people have never forgiven him. It's absolute bullshit. Lepselter came to my room that morning and nearly punched me across the face and said, "Let's go." Outside of physically punching me in the face and throwing me in the car—which is very difficult to do to somebody who is high—he did everything he could to get me out of that room that day. He made it very clear: "Sid, if you don't leave it's over." It's easy for people to say that he should have knocked me out, he should have tied me up, but I was high and I wasn't having it. Lepselter's gotten a raw deal over that. I was in my thirties, I was a father, and he's not my babysitter; he's my agent. He tried; he really did try. He could have walked me into my hotel room, kissed me goodnight, put me into bed, and 15 minutes later or when he was in his elevator back to his hotel room, I would have gotten dressed and gone out. I was in a hotel in a casino in

Atlantic City—it's 24 hours a day! Unless he slept in the same room with me, there was nothing he could have done to stop me that night. That angel and devil were going to battle that night, and the devil was going to win.

I never made it back for the Giants game that Sunday, and again they had to throw Chris Carlin on the air. I finally got back late Sunday night. On Monday morning I was on the way to the station with my wife, and I knew I was in trouble. I think my wife thought that maybe we could talk to Chernoff and save my job. On the way there, we were on the George Washington Bridge and got a call from Chernoff. He basically said, "Turn the car around; it ain't gonna happen." He also told my wife that in all the years on radio—and he's worked with everybody from Stern to Imus to Scott Muni, all these fucking legends and greats—he never had to say goodbye to a guy with more talent and never felt worse in his career than he felt that morning.

And with that, I was gone. A week later I was pulling out of my driveway at 5:00 AM in Tenafly, New Jersey, with no job. We went down to Florida to live with Danielle's cousin. We stopped in North Carolina to see her dad for a couple of days. I knew I had some friends at a small station down in Florida, and thought I had a chance to work with those guys. When I pulled out of my driveway a week after I was fired, I didn't take I-95 straight down to Florida like I usually did. This time we took the more scenic route. I went through the mountains in Asheville, North Carolina. My wife was sleeping in the front, and my daughter, Ava, who was 17 months, was sleeping in the back, and I just started crying, because it had occurred to me I was 38 years old and I just had the opportunity of a lifetime and it was gone, which was bad enough. I was on *Imus*, I had the midday show, I was hosting the Giants. People loved me—and people hated me, too. Then it also occurred to me, I've got a baby in the back seat and a wife who's been with me forever and I just had no idea what I was going to do. No idea. It was a harrowing fucking realization driving in the hills of North

Carolina. The tears started coming down, and I could not stop it. It came out of nowhere: *Oh my God, what have I done?*

Some people say that the only guy we developed at the FAN was Joe Benigno. But the guys on the inside will tell you that the biggest talent they ever developed at the FAN was me. I had the real chance of being a fucking major, major superstar. And then it was gone. Gone. Fucking gone.

WE NOW INTERRUPT OUR REGULARLY SCHEDULED BROADCAST
FOR A WORD FROM…

MARK CHERNOFF, Program director, WFAN

I knew Sid was working at WNEW, and I can remember an incident. We were doing a WFAN remote in 2000 with Mike and Chris, and I see this guy standing in hockey gear, basically. He was wearing a Rangers jersey, and he almost looked like he was in uniform, ready to be a goalie. I knew what Sid looked like, because I had seen pictures of him. We kind of just got into a conversation, and he said, "You know, I'm doing sports, I love sports, and the thing I'd love to do most is that I always wanted to work at the FAN." I knew he was a real personality. I said, "Sid, I'll get back in touch with you. Let me think about things." At the time I was looking for somebody to do something with Imus. Warner Wolf was doing sports with Imus because Mike Breen had left to do the NBA full time. Warner really didn't want to work five days a week because he was also doing TV. He was doing the 11:00 PM news. I went into Imus and asked if he'd ever heard of Sid and he said not really. I played him some stuff and he said, "The kid sounds like he's got some talent." I asked if maybe I could bring him in for a day to see if he liked him. Imus was a little bit reluctant but said "Sure, go ahead." I brought him in and he loved him. He thought he was hysterical. And before you know it, we wound up having Sid do sports a couple of days a week.

Eventually Warner's TV job became so time consuming that he really couldn't do radio anymore, and Sid developed into the everyday guy doing sports in the morning for Imus. I was also looking for a midday host to partner up with Jody McDonald. So we also had Sid do a couple of fill-in shows at the time. After Suzyn Waldman decided she no longer could do the grind of being on every day, I obviously needed a second midday host, I put Sid on with Jody, and lo and behold I now had a midday show with the two of them, and Sid was also doing the sports in the morning with Imus.

He was just very entertaining. He was opinionated. I started to hear some of the things after a while that came out of his mouth, and I scratched my head. He knew a lot about sports. He could do a sportscast on *Imus* really without any paper other than just having the scores of the games. During the day he was just a really good sports talk show host. He had a way with callers that was very good. He was opinionated, and he knew all the subject matter, whether it was baseball, basketball, hockey, football, or college basketball. We had a lot of fun, we did a bunch of remotes, and he was very personable. The sales people enjoyed working with him because he was always easy to talk to. If you told him about a product and it was something he was interested in, he was more than willing to do the commercial and do a nice live read. He just had a nice, really good way about him around the radio station.

I didn't know a whole lot about Sid. I got to work about 5:45 AM and he usually was here earlier than that, but one day he was pulling in when I was and he had all kinds of what looked like tire stuff all over him. He said something about changing a tire. As it turned out, that's not what happened, but I didn't know that. I listened to the excuse. After a while, sometimes there were these patterns of stories that I questioned. He was late once and I threatened him, "We're going to fire you if you're ever late again," and he was never late after that. There was the one incident, he blamed it on a flat tire. I said, "Why didn't you call if you had a flat tire?" It's not like Sid didn't have a cell phone. His issues came mostly when he was out of town. One was at a Super Bowl, another time was when he was in Cleveland. I'm not sure he was actually trying to fake me out, but I was finally starting to get it.

There were a few incidents on the air that were a little outrageous, some more harmful than others. He had an incident early on when he made a really terrible remark about the Williams sisters, and I did suspend him right away. Actually, I was ready to fire him, because I thought it was so bad. We, among other things, had him write a letter to both Williams sisters, to their father, and also to their agent. I said, "You know what, as much as I think he's talented, I can't have people say stuff like this on the radio." Imus said to me, "You know, I've done a lot of stupid things on the radio and I haven't been fired. Well, in one case I did get fired, but you know what, I think he deserves a second chance." By Imus saying people do deserve a second chance, I did re-hire him. I didn't technically fire him, but I had basically said, "You're going to be fired." Imus absolutely saved his job.

I never regretted it. I think Sid is really talented. He's had issues through the years. I warned him a million times. He did go to rehab, but I don't think he took it seriously. It was somewhere up in Lafayette, New Jersey, in Sussex County. I remember going to the Forum Diner on Route 4. It was me, Sid, and Danielle, and I basically said "Okay, you're all cleaned up, you're fine, you're doing better." Sid sometimes can be a con artist. He's got that poker face, where you really want to believe that he means it when he says that he's going to be fine and he's going to do all the right things. I just got disappointed a lot by the fact that he didn't follow up on that. That's been my biggest disappointment. He made some other dumb remarks on the air; one was about Kylie Minogue. That was horrible, and because of that incident we actually took him off the *Imus* show. Imus basically said, "I've had it with you. You can't say stupid things like that." And then the last straw was when he didn't show up for a Giants pregame show.

He was doing something with *FHM* magazine, and he and his agent were going to go down to Atlantic City to collect the cash or the check, whatever it was. I had told Sid that Friday, "You better be here for the pregame show. If you're not, you're done." I warned him, "I'm not putting up with any shenanigans any more. You're done. You need to be taught a lesson, so just don't go." He said, "I'm going to go, and I'll be fine." I said, "You'd better be back." I thought maybe he thought better of it, but he did go. I remember saying to Mark Lepselter, "I really don't think it's a good idea for Sid to go to Atlantic City. He's not going with his wife. You're taking him down there." He was like, "Don't worry. I'll take care of him. He'll be with me the whole time." Well, he was with him *most* of the time. Most of the time is not all of the time. And all I can tell you is, I went to Giants Stadium, waiting for him to do the pregame show. I got there about 10:00 AM. The pregame show went on at 11:30, so Sid usually got there around 10:30. I didn't see him. It's 10:45; I didn't see him. I happened to see his father in the parking lot and I said, "Mr. Rosenberg, have you seen Sid?" because I figured maybe they'd come together. He looked at me and said no. And I could see his heart sinking as I was talking to him.

I'm thinking, *Oh God, this doesn't look good.* Well, maybe his cell phone broke and he'll be here late, just in time to do the show. He didn't show up. Not only didn't show up, he didn't call. Nothing. I heard nothing from him until the next day when he basically called and said, "Well, I was in Atlantic City," and I said, "You're fired. That's all there is to it. I warned you. I told you not to go." It was very hard, but if I say I'm going to do something, I have to do it. What am I going to say? I'll give you another chance now? Then people don't ever believe you. If you say you're going to do something, you have to do it. I was really disappointed in him. I couldn't believe he could do this to himself and his family and his job. I called and said, "Don't come in, you're not working." He said, "Yeah, I'm going to work." I said, "No, you're not working. I told you; you're fired."

You tend to give more chances because you see that talent and you hope that they'll straighten themselves out because you hate to give up that talent. Before that, I was looking at him having a place at FAN very long term, absolutely. I never say never to basically anything. We've talked in the past about things. I think he's doing much better, and every time I see him in Florida he seems to be fine. I hope and think things are okay, but I'm not there. He's his own worst enemy. He's a character, no doubt about it, one of the more colorful guys out there.

WE NOW INTERRUPT OUR REGULARLY SCHEDULED BROADCAST
FOR A WORD FROM. . .

MIKE BREEN, Former *Imus* sportscaster,
Lead NBA play-by-play, ABC, ESPN, New York Knicks

Sid has a way of pissing people off, but he also has a way of making you forgive him and forget very quickly. I've never had any kind of problem with him, but I know people who he's pissed off. He's a charming guy; he's absolutely charming. I firmly believe he has a really good heart. He's a really good guy; he just gets a little crazed sometimes and tries to make statements that either outrage people or just to get them to perk up. Sometimes he means what he says, but other times he's just doing it for effect. He's really talented. If he could just harness it and be a little more politically correct he could hold a job longer.

Replacing me on *Imus* was Patrick McEnroe, and they brought in a bunch of different guys. I heard all the people that filled in on *Imus*, and right away you could see how talented Sid was. There's the expression, "having a real radio presence." He has a *great* radio presence. It's partly his voice; it's partly the authoritative way he talks. Whether what he's saying is so off the mark or whether it's exactly right, he talks with such conviction. And he just has an upbeat, bubbly personality. I combine that and say that's what a great radio presence is. He's always had that. So he's one of those guys, whether you like what he says or you're disgusted by what he says, who you're listening to because he has that presence. Everybody that's worked with him knows that. The other thing, too, is he just has so much damn energy and he has it all the time, whether he's doing morning drive, whether he's doing overnights. Whatever it is, he comes with energy to whatever job he has, and that's a gift, too.

It's very easy to get caught up in trying to please Imus, because he likes when whoever's on his show says outrageous things that are going to bring about a controversy or get people talking. But you have to have some self-control and realize you're on the air. In a lot of ways, that's one of the hardest things about working on that show. You're all sitting around, a whole bunch of you talking, and sometimes you really do forget that it's on the air, because it becomes like family. You're sitting in there with your family and you're going back and forth with each other, and you just got to be careful with what you say sometimes.

We all think we know where to draw the line. Unfortunately, Sid doesn't know that frequently. Sometimes he just goes way over, it and he does that for effect. I really don't believe he does it in any way, shape, or fashion that is in any way mean-spirited. He likes to get people to laugh with him, and sometimes he thinks certain ways are a good way to make them laugh. But he also has to remember that whatever he says has an impact. There are many, many people out there listening to him, and he just needs to have a better editor in his head sometimes.

When I was on *Imus* I would occasionally get a call from my father and he'd say, "Hey, easy does it there, fella." I tried to be a little more careful. You really have to be on your guard all the time, because some of the things that are said around you while you're doing your sportscast can easily draw you into stuff. Sometimes you get caught up in the back and forth, but I don't think I ever came close. This might sound silly, but with the Williams sisters and Kylie Minogue, Sid meant those things to be funny. It obviously was so inappropriate in both cases and he deserved to get punished for it. You just hope that he learns from it. But I don't think there's a mean-spirited bone in his body. He has to realize words can really hurt and words can do damage—even when you're trying to do it in a satirical, humorous way—they still hurt to the people they're aimed at.

He's sincere in how apologetic he is after he does it. It's not an excuse, but if it starts happening one too many times then you say, "Okay, well maybe he's not so sincere," but I really do believe he was.

I go on with him often, and he's terrific. He doesn't take himself too seriously, and he knows that he's entertaining, that he has to entertain. To me, he combines the entertainment and at the same time sports information that makes for a really good radio show. He's not a know-it-all by any stretch. He has a great fan's perspective, like he's still a fan. I love that about him. He doesn't just do the straight "What about them defensively?" or "Do you think they have enough help at the backup point guard?" He has fun when he does it. You talk about a lot of different things, and it's like having a conversation with a buddy when you're a guest on his show. You actually look forward to it. I do a lot of the shows and they're all good in their own way, but I actually look forward to going on with Sid because it's fun.

He's a big hugger; he likes to hug. You see him at a press conference, where everybody's so professional and acting accordingly and he comes up and he gives you a big hug, and he makes you tell him that you love him because he's insecure and he wants to know. But you do. You like hugging him and, you do love him because he's just this big, happy-go-lucky guy. He loves what he does. You can't help but like him when you get to know him. I remember when he first started on *Imus*, I didn't like a lot of the stuff, I thought it was too lowbrow. I thought one of the reasons the *Imus* show was always so popular and influential with advertisers is that it had an intelligent humor to it. I thought when he first got there he was just trying to do dirty-joke type stuff and I remember talking to Bernard McGuirk about him. Bernard was really the first one to say to me, "No, no, the guy is really smart and he's really good. The guy is terrific." Now, Bernard likes controversial people on the show so that was part of it, because Bernard could play off a lot of what Sid said. He spotted him early and said "Give him a chance," and the more I listened to Sid the more I could see a method to the madness.

It's like a player who's overly emotional, who gets in guys' faces, like a Nate Robinson of the Knicks. If you take away his showboating, his flair, and the stuff that sometimes pisses off teammates, sometimes annoys coaches, certainly annoys opponents, when you take that away, that's part of his strength. I think it's the same thing with Sid. You take away a little bit of the edge—he's not a guy who's hesitant or gun-shy, he shoots from the hip, he speaks with raw emotion, and that's who he is. Not to say he still doesn't have to be careful. It's that fine line and making sure you don't go over it but at the same time maintaining who you are.

Trading Barbs with the King of All Media

I went back to work for Don Imus in 2000. The Rangers put on a hockey game for Christopher Reeve's charity every year at Madison Square Garden. They hired radio guys as the coaches for the teams. I'm a die-hard Rangers fan, so I jumped at the chance. The teams were filled with celebrities and former hockey players like Ron Duguay, Kim Alexis, Jason Priestley, and Rick Moranis. One year Gary Dell'Abate was on my team. That was a big thrill because I was a big Howard Stern fan—Gary Dell'Abate is of course "Baba Booey," Stern's producer. I remember I even put him on the ice for the last shift along with Kenny Albert and Rick Moranis. Needless to say, he was all excited about that. That day we really forged a friendship. We kept in touch via e-mail here and there and when I was working for the FAN because he's a huge sports fan.

Gary's parents lived in West Palm Beach, and in 2006 his father died. So he came down to kind of get his mother situated, and e-mailed me out of the blue. He said, "Hey, I'm going to be down in West Palm for a couple of days. The Mets are playing the Dodgers tonight in the first round of the playoffs. If you're free tonight, let's watch the game." That was the year the Mets went on to beat the Dodgers but lost to the Cardinals in the NLCS. So we went out to a bar and grill and watched the Mets and the

Dodgers. We sat there for about four hours, even after the game was over, just bullshitting.

He kept asking me questions about what happened with Imus, what happened with FAN. I went over it all: the crazy things that happened over the years, the controversial suspensions, the firings. He was amazed. He just sat there wide-eyed the whole time. I was thinking, *Wait a second, you run* The Howard Stern Show*, and this is somewhat interesting to you?* He was like, "Oh my God, are you kidding me? This is great. Howard would love to have you on." At the time, I had already left WFAN. There was a feeling out there, that now that I was gone from the FAN, I hated everybody—Imus, Mike and the Mad Dog, everybody. That of course wasn't really true. I think Dell'Abate figured I'd come on *The Howard Stern Show* and tell these crazy stories, but at the same time I think he thought I was going to badmouth Don—which of course Stern loves to do, because he still hates Imus.

Sure enough, three days later Gary called me back and told me that Howard wanted me on. It was Thanksgiving 2006, so I flew to New York and spent Thanksgiving weekend with my family. That Monday morning I work up and went to Sirius to do *The Howard Stern Show*. The first day I was on *Imus* I had been really nervous, but I don't think I was ever as nervous as I was when I walked into the studios with Stern. I sat there on the couch and was like 10 feet away from him. I had seen Howard at a Knicks game once and at a restaurant in the city before. We'd never had any real conversation before then.

To me, he's the greatest of all time. How many guys in my father's generation loved and revered Mickey Mantle? He's that caliber for me. I'm a radio junkie. My life is radio, and he's the best of all time. I knew Imus, I knew Mike Francesa, and these other big names around sports talk radio, but I really didn't know Howard all that well. It was intimidating.

It was the week Michael Richards, Kramer from *Seinfeld*, got in trouble for saying the N-word in a comedy club. The first thing

Howard said to me was, "All right, Sid, everybody knows about you and your career at the FAN and you got in trouble with the Venus comment and the Serena comment. Looking back at what happened with Michael Richards this week, you're a guy who said crazy stuff like that. Do you think he's a racist?" I said yes. He asked me why, when I've said the same types of things. I said, "Yeah, but I was only kidding." He started laughing, and we got off to a very good start.

I sat there with Stern for about 45 minutes. Howard asked me about some of the things I had done on *Imus*. He brought up the Kylie Minogue thing and said, "Are you fucking crazy?" I said, "Wait a second, you're Howard Stern?" He brought up Venus Williams; he brought up all the stuff that got me fired. He tried to get me to badmouth Don and I wouldn't do it that day. I said, "Listen, truth be told, I think Don, takes a lot of shit and not all of it is his fault." I was a little nervous at the time that Howard would get angry with me if I didn't really bash Imus, but he didn't. He was totally cool. We talked about my drug history, my drinking, my gambling history. It was a pretty cool conversation, and he thanked me.

I was told he was a germaphobe, one of those guys who doesn't like to touch people or shake hands. So when the interview was over I fully expected him to just wave and say good-bye, but he actually called me over to where he was sitting and shook my hand. That really surprised me.

My wife and my father came with me. They sat in the green room while I was in there getting grilled by Howard about my career and all the stupid stuff I had done. I couldn't see my wife and my father, but I knew a couple of times we were going into some talk that was a bit rough, stuff that was probably tough on my wife. At one point Robin Quivers said, "You smoked crack and went to work?" which I hadn't, and I denied. I found out my wife actually started to cry at that point. It ended up being kind of rough for my wife and my father.

* * *

In the summer of 2008 I got a phone call from one of the guys at Howard TV, which is a psy channel. It has all original programming, such as *Wack Pack Bowling*, *Strip Beer Pong*, and *Stump the Booey*. It also shows highlights from his actual radio show, which they film as well.

They asked me to be the host of *Wack Pack Bowling*. Howard has a group called the Wack Packers. They're all mentally challenged people or they have problems. We were going to tape four episodes in one day at a bowling alley in Harlem, and they were all on hand that day. The bowling alley is on the third floor of this building in Harlem. The elevator opened up and there they all were, every one of these Wack Packers. There was Bettlejuice, a black midget with no teeth. He's fucking hilarious. He's the funniest guy there. Elephant Boy is another one of the characters, and Jeff the Drunk is just a raging alcoholic who can barely function. Gary the Retard and Wendy the Retard were there—all the famous Wack Packers. They were all sitting there as the elevator opened, which was quite an eye-opener at 8:30 in the morning.

These are people who had called in to *The Howard Stern Show* for years and years and years, people who are mentally disabled or challenged or however you want to put it, who have become regulars on the show over the years. And one day Stern just decided to call them the Wack Pack. So we got them together and had them bowl against each other, for a grand prize of just over $2,000 and a $5 trophy. Watching them just trying to fucking bowl was hilarious. They actually had to use the gutter guards that they use for little kids. There was a lot of physical comedy on display and you're not supposed to laugh at them, but of course Howard loves that shit. All these guys were bowling against each other, and each one was worse than the one before.

I used to host a lot of TV shows, and have appeared on a lot of of them. Usually, you get there in the morning and they've got bagels, they've got coffee, all the regular stuff. Only on Howard is there vodka at 8:00 in the morning—and these Wack Packers were just drinking up a storm. We taped all four episodes, and it was a blast. Howard brought me on his show to promote it, and he was very, very complimentary to me on a bunch of occasions. It actually did pretty well for them.

Doing anything with Howard Stern is a fucking great time. Yeah, of course anybody out there who's got a hard-on for me uses that against me, but look, the fact is, I'm not hosting *Meet the Press* anytime soon. Was Rudy Giuliani on my shows during the election? Yeah. Was Joe Lieberman? Yeah. Have I talked to some of the more famous politicians and guys who covered politics? Yeah. Does Chuck Todd, the NBC White House Chief Correspondent, come on my show? Yeah, he absolutely does. He's an admitted friend of mine. So if I'm hosting *Wack Pack Bowling*, will there be people out there that will say that's kind of inconsistent? Sure, but that's what Imus deals with all the time. He goes from talking to the president to doing bits with me, Bernie, and Rob.

I used to listen to Howard almost every single day. I can't remember a day when I didn't laugh listening to Stern. There were days when I laughed so hard I had to stop my car. I think he's a brilliant interviewer. Imus is great, too. He can interview the President of the United States, but Imus doesn't have the range. When I used to be on Don's show, there'd be a hit movie out and I'd say, "Hey, let's get this guy on the show." And Don would say, "Nobody fucking knows who that guy is." Imus can't sit down with someone like Kevin James. Give Imus the president and he's great, or prepare Imus and he can interview anybody. Howard, however, does have the range, whether he sits down with a porn star or an actress or dignitary. A while back he did an interview with Cloris Leachman, who is like a fucking 1,000 years old, and it was the funniest thing I've ever heard. I can name dozens and dozens of times when I heard the name of a guest scheduled to appear and

I'd think, *Yeah, that's not going to be all that good* and then afterward, *I don't know how the fuck he does it.* That's what it's all about. For me, he's just on a totally different level.

WE NOW INTERRUPT OUR REGULARLY SCHEDULED BROADCAST FOR A WORD FROM...

GARY DELL'ABATE, Producer, *The Howard Stern Show*

I had to take my mom down to Florida after my father died. My dad had been dead for two months, and my mom wouldn't leave, wouldn't go back to Florida. I kept saying "Mom, we have to go. You can't stay here forever. At some point you have to go home." I said, "I'll tell you what, I'll fly back with you so you don't have to walk into the house alone." All of a sudden I realize it's a Saturday night and the Mets are playing the Dodgers in the playoffs—this is 2006. My mother doesn't even like baseball. I should have been watching this game with my dad. I was all bummed out.

Sid is stupid like me. He acts like he doesn't know anything, but he's got a fucking great memory. He called me on my cell phone once while I was coaching my kid's football team, and he was looking for Artie Lange. I didn't know Sid. I knew he worked for Imus and he seemed like a good guy. I knew *of* him. I would hear people talk about him and hear the trouble he got into, and some of it would make me laugh. We talked on the phone a bunch of times, but I never hung out with him. I e-mailed him to tell him I'd be down in Florida and that I wanted to watch the Mets game and he said, "Come hang out with me."

Sid takes me to this place—and this is what's so great about Sid—literally, the name of the place is "The Neighborhood Bar." It's about a 30-minute drive from my mom's house. I meet him there. I always thought the guy was a nut. His wife and his daughter show up there for a little while, they have a little dessert, then they leave, and Sid and I watch the game. And we start talking, and he starts telling me these stories. "I was high out of my mind on crack," and "I was in Detroit," and something about a blackout. Every time he tells me another story it's more outrageous than the one before. I said, "Sid, man, would you talk about these stories on the radio?" Sometimes you get people who have good stories and don't know how to tell them. Sometimes you have people who have good stories and won't tell them.

Ten minutes into dinner I'm thinking, "Sid would be great on the air." The stories were really out there, really crazy shit. We had a great time that night, and the Mets won. they beat the Dodgers. My job is to book guests, to see who can contribute to the show. I was aware Sid wanted to be on the show because I had heard he was a huge fan, but I don't think he asked me to go out that night to try to get on the show. He was just being himself.

That's what I do when I talk to people. That's how it happened with Artie Lange. Norm Macdonald of *Saturday Night Live* was coming on with Howard, and Artie came with him and was in the green room. Norm Macdonald said, "Artie punched his manager and he was on coke and the police arrested him and he took a swing at a cop." I said, "You're kidding! Would you talk about it on the air?" and Artie goes, "Sure." With Sid I totally recognized right away, not only does the guy have good stories, but he can tell a good story. I went back and I said to Howard, "I spent a weekend with this guy, and he's a fucking panic. I think he'd be a good guest." So we booked him as a guest on the show.

He was off the *Imus* show at that point, and that was an interesting part of it too. He was more than willing to talk about how Mark Chernoff and Imus threw him under the bus and how they fucked him over, how they knew exactly what he was and what he would say and all of a sudden people would look at him and go, "Uh huh" and pretended they didn't know him—which is sort of our story with Stern. We've been down that road 1,000 times.

He went on with Howard in the studio. He took some shots at Imus. He could have done a lot worse and probably should have. I knew he wanted to get on bad. His name had been kicked around a couple of times. Howard would talk about him, his name was in the papers, and he was definitely on Howard's radar. He was all about it, man.

When he was doing his Miami show it was very nice. He would have me call in like once every two or three months. I was thinking, *If Sid's got me calling in he really must be desperate for a taste of New York.* We'd talk about the Mets and the Jets, because I'm a huge fan of both, talk a little bit of hockey, whatever. Sid's got a good ear. It was just two New York guys talking sports.

He's a fucking nut. He'll make you crazy. He would call me and send me e-mails. Chris Russo got his own channel on Sirius, and for some reason Sid got it in his mind that it was his God-given right to be on Mad Dog's channel. Sid's one of those guys—I love him, but he loves to be a victim, loves to be the underdog, loves to pick a fight. He had it in his mind that Mad Dog didn't want him on his channel because he didn't like him from FAN, which may or may not have been true. But Sid had it in his mind that Mad Dog had to put him on, because he *had* to, because he's Sid Rosenberg. He would send me these angry e-mails, like, *What the fuck is wrong with Russo?* At one point I was ready to say to him, *Maybe he just doesn't want to have you on. Move on.* He gets so angry and so passionate. I went to people at Sirius in a variety of different places, places where I thought Sid would be a good asset, but I think a lot of people were scared of him. I got to meet the straight, not high, very well-behaved Sid Rosenberg, but his reputation precedes him. Even on satellite radio you still have rules.

I always wondered why he couldn't get back to New York radio, but the problem is there's really only one sports station in New York, and he sort of burned that bridge. Mark Chernoff runs the ship. I've known Mark a long time. Mark used to be my program director. Mark is a really good guy, but Mark is a straight arrow. He's got only so much patience for that, probably a lot less than some other people. On *Stern* we might have a little bit more patience; we walk the edge a little bit more. Mark runs a pretty tight ship, so he probably just ran out of patience. Sid's going to have to wait for Mark to die to get back to FAN, but he's a natural for FAN. He's New York.

WE NOW INTERRUPT OUR REGULARLY SCHEDULED BROADCAST
FOR A WORD FROM...

JACKIE "THE JOKEMAN" MARTLING,
Comedian, formerly of *The Howard Stern Show*

I don't know anything about Imus. I never listened to *Imus* and I don't know a lot about sports, but somebody booked me on Sid's radio show. I was doing a show at the New York Comedy Club in Boca Raton, and somehow I got hooked into being on with Sid. I know I had heard of him, but I wasn't too aware of him, and I didn't know if he knew me. I went down to do his show, and he was one of those guys—we had one of those rapports like the second we met, and we made each other laugh. He got me and I got him. He realized right away I could be lewd and funny and dirty without getting us in trouble, so he immediately realized he could breathe easy. He knew I did 15 years of Stern and never went over the line in the way you shouldn't. When he knew that, he could have fun and relax and really laugh with me. He's just a real good egg, a funny guy, and a hard worker. He's a good soul, a likeable New York Jew.

Because of my connection with Stern, he was a lot more aware of me than I was of him but he only knew of me as the guy that Howard painted and I'm a lot different guy than the guy who was painted on the show. I'm a lot nicer and a lot smarter than people envisioned from when I was on *Stern*, so I think he was very pleasantly surprised and we got to be friends. He's a wild man and he certainly doesn't need anybody else on the air with him ever, but like everybody else, it just makes it more fun for him.

You talk about stepping over the line—Sid redrew the line and stomped on it. The fact that there's a line at all is so absolutely absurd. If somebody's listening to a comedy show, it's a comedy show. There's so much horror in the world. If people are trying to create horror, that's bad. The age-old argument, Gershon Legman's thing—you can watch somebody chop each other up on television, but you can't watch two people having sex. Murdering someone's against the law and making love with somebody isn't against the law, but murdering someone on TV is allowed but having sex with somebody on TV isn't. It is so exactly backward and it's the age-old argument that's so ponderous it's even absurd to go through it because it's so old, but it's still as wrong as it ever was.

When it comes to race and stuff like that, it's all in the spirit. Everything is the ear of the listener. What you don't like, I like. What's your line and what's my line? I go to a comedy club, and I like the midget jokes, but I don't like when you do the Jewish jokes, and I like the black jokes, but I don't like it when you do the fat girl jokes because I'm fat. C'mon, we're trying to relax and have fun and have entertainment. There is no such thing as bad taste if people are laughing. That's what I believe. The spirit is everything. I do "Stump the Jokeman" in my shows and I say horrible things to these women and to these guys, but I'm breaking balls. It's like the 2010 version of Groucho Marx. He'd say things that were insulting, but they're not insulting. It's in the flavor of what's going on.

I'm not an *Opie and Anthony* fan. I've never listened to their show, but they once sent a guy and girl to St. Patrick's Cathedral. The couple made love there, and they fired Opie and Anthony. And it was just pressure from the Catholic diocese. It's just absurd. First of all, if you're not a Catholic, St. Patrick's is nothing but a building. Sure, if you're Catholic, to you it's a church. A temple is this to you. if you're an African and that log is what you respect, then that log is your church. Whatever. This guy and this girl, they didn't go and set fire to the place, they didn't go and chop it up, they went and had sex, which in the grand scheme of things is love, which is what religion and Catholicism and everything else is supposed to totally be about. You can look at it as disrespectful, but in the grand scheme of things is was just goofy. I could see saying, "Listen guys, you're not thinking. That isn't right. that's going to rub people wrong." But to fire them under pressure, things are out of hand. I'm sure that when Imus fired Sid it was under pressure. Most of those guys felt like what he did wasn't anything that onerous. But you have to bow to the pressure. Meanwhile, nobody's willing to stand up and say, "C'mon, lighten up. Jesus Christ!"

The Rutgers thing when Imus got fired—I don't know if the word "innocent" applies but he certainly wasn't calling the girls whores. I remember the first time I was watching Johnny Carson, years ago, and he said, "Yeah, I saw such and such, and I got to tell you, that sucks." That really struck me. I was old enough that I know that "that sucks dick" became "that sucks." When you say something "sucks" to me you're saying, "That sucks dick." What it means now is "that stinks," but the genesis of it is, it sucks dick. If you say that people are "hos" you're saying it—but you're not saying they're whores any more than Carson was saying going to that play last night sucked dick. You can find problems wherever you want to look.

I know Sid loves the *Stern* show and the whole thing. He's a character. He's funny, but what's better about him is how unique he is. Not that a loud Jew is unique, but he just is. He's outspoken, he's a mile-a-minute, and he's fun. He's a different type guy. He's in your face. He dances to his own drummer, and being that kind of guy, I love that. I'm not saying he's funnier than me. Fuck him. I would discuss his demons if I wasn't so busy battling mine. I quit drinking eight years ago, and I'm still dealing with it. He seems to be weathering it fine. Of course, I don't know that. As we speak, he could have a needle in his arm.

Like Ralphie Cifaretto, with a Microphone

I have a really good friend named Michael Sullivan. He worked with the *Sopranos* cast, driving around James Gandolfini, Tony Sirico, and all those guys. He helped them with their daily errands and kind of became their Girl Friday. Sullivan and I had been friendly for 30 years. My next-door neighbor Joe Iovine was friendly with the Sullivan boys and, as it turned out, one of my favorite restaurants in America—a roast beef place called Brennan & Carr—is Sullivan's place. It's one of the oldest and best restaurants in Brooklyn, located right on the corner of Avenue U and Nostrand Avenue, and it's been there for 100 years.

When Sullivan became friends with all these *Sopranos* guys, little by little he would introduce me to those guys. I talked to them on the phone, they came on the radio show, and we'd hang out. They'd come on the *Imus* show and come in and say hello to me. Imus loved *The Sopranos*, Mike Francesa loved it too, and I got to know these guys personally. Back in May 2004 I went on the air on *Imus* and said, "Look, I'm telling ya, Adriana is going to get whacked next week." Imus said, "C'mon, how do you know that?" even though everyone kind of surmised that was going to happen because it looked like she was going to leave the show. No one had told me anything—it wasn't like Steve Schirripa or Tony Sirico or

Sullivan had spilled the beans to me—but I went on *Imus* and said "I'm telling you I-Man, I got it from a good source." But I always said shit like that, "I got it from a good source." I always wanted to make it seem like I was like Francesa, like I'm *it*, you know? I had no idea. There were always rumors about who was going to get whacked. I was keeping up with the stories and I just figured, "This bitch is about to get knocked off the show."

Wouldn't you know it, the next week she gets whacked, that Sunday night! It gets back to David Chase and all the *Sopranos* guys. Chase was furious. Schirripa was furious. All these guys were pissed with me because they really thought that some way or another I got the information and I revealed the spoiler.

The last season they opened up their season with a premiere at Radio City. They had a red carpet, and they showed the first two episodes there. I was invited to go. The very last episode aired live at the Hard Rock Hotel and Casino in Miami, so I saw all those guys there. They're all huge sports fans. Schirripa and Sirico loved me on the FAN and on *Imus*. Imus had Schirripa on all the time, and he had Vinnie Curatola, the guy who played the New York crime boss Johnny Sack. James Gandolfini doesn't like Imus. I guess Imus said something bad about him on the air once about him being a fat cokehead or something that and Gandolfini never forgave him.

TV has always been one of my passions, and I love *The Sopranos*. I think it's the best show of all time. It's as simple as that. It's difficult to compare it to the comedies. *Seinfeld* and *All in the Family* are two of the best comedies of all time, in my opinion. But in terms of drama, I think *The Sopranos* is the best show I've ever seen. There are a lot of shows that I have watched over the years that I loved. I loved *NYPD Blue*, and I loved *Hill Street Blues* early on, but *The Sopranos* had everything. It had the excitement, it had the violence, it made you laugh, it made you cry, made you think, and the acting was brilliant.

There never was and never will be a phenomenon like *The Sopranos*. I felt like I was in it. I knew the guys. Schirripa is a friend. Tony Sirico is a good friend. Mike Sullivan is a dear friend. Michael Imperioli and I were together on occasion. Even though I never got the chance to be in it, I really was, because it was *me*. Those guys in that show, I owed guys like that money my whole life. Let's be honest; when those characters came on the screen people would say, "That's funny," but every once in a while I would sit there and feel sick to my stomach. The normal person, the everyday guy, doesn't deal with bookmakers and mafia. But I'm sitting there thinking, *I know a guy like that*. It's one thing to watch *The Sopranos* just for the acting and the quality of writing; it's another when you think, *Holy shit, I've been in that situation more than once.*

Look, September 11th was a tragedy for the whole country. But to me—and I know people around the country get mad at me for this—I took it more personally because I was in New York. I know people died in Shanksville, Pennsylvania, and I know many people died in the Pentagon. And I know that even if nobody died in your home state you still take it personally. I get it. But no matter what anybody tells me, living a couple of blocks from the World Trade Center and having friends who died upstairs that day, having the smoke billow into my apartment on 21st Street and 8th Avenue that morning, I took it more personally. Three thousand people died where I lived my life for 36 of my 43 years. And *The Sopranos* is kind of the same thing. Those are my guys. Those were my guys on the show, and those are my guys in real life. Growing up in Brooklyn and going to Poly Prep and Bay Ridge and hanging out in Bensonhurst, those were my guys. For every *Sopranos* character, I knew the real-life counterpart. It's just more personal.

WE NOW INTERRUPT OUR REGULARLY SCHEDULED BROADCAST
FOR A WORD FROM...

STEVE SCHIRRIPA, Actor, Bobby Bacala on *The Sopranos*

Can I say what a fucking retard Sid is? He's a nice guy who's a little fucking screwy. He's a very lovable, intelligent guy who's got a little screw loose there. He's all over the map. I don't think he's a bad guy, otherwise I wouldn't talk to him, because when I don't like somebody I just don't bother with them. There is something about Sid that's very likeable.

During the run of *The Sopranos* I had done *Imus* a whole lot of times. I became one of Imus' guys, and Sid was always very supportive. Sid was always looking to help you. You're on one of the biggest radio shows in the country. Imus could be prickly, but he was always nice to me, and I think that's kind of because of Sid, too. Sid knew me and Bernard McGuirk knew me. Going to work with Imus can't be easy every day, but Imus was very good to Sid.

Sid was very knowledgeable. He was a big *Sopranos* fan, so when I would come in in the morning he was always trying to find out what's going on. He always thought he was kind of in the inner circle. He knew a bunch of the guys. I think one time he may have either guessed or knew something about a storyline and said something about Adriana getting whacked. I don't know if he did get inside information, I don't know if he really did have it—which is hard to believe, but it's possible—or he just guessed it. But guys were annoyed, like *Shut your mouth*. One thing about *The Sopranos*, it was extremely, extremely secretive, and we were very protective of that. David Chase was protective of the storylines, and it went down the line. If anybody was suspected of blowing the whistle or giving out a storyline, guys would be pissed. For a while, guys got annoyed with Sid. That's the way to get ostracized from the show. That's the way to get yourself killed off the show. If it gets found out that you said the wrong thing in an interview—purposely or by accident—that could have been the next episode, you're in the trunk of a car.

There's something endearing about Sid. He's a quick talker. Most of the guys we'd shoo away, but he's a Brooklyn guy. He knew a lot about the show, and he was always talking a million miles a minute. He was okay. Sid was on our side. But there's no filter system with Sid. What pops in his head comes out of his mouth. I think that's the problem. Sometimes it's brilliant; sometimes it gets his ass in the wringer.

Sid's also the kind of guy...he's like herpes. He doesn't go away. He just keeps coming back. He somehow just keeps on fucking popping up. For a while there he just kept popping up everywhere. We're at an event, a charity event, you would see him everywhere. Some of the guys on the show thought Sid was a little kooky.

Sid was always a welcoming face when you walked into *Imus* at 6:30 AM, and he's talking a million miles a minute. I'm from Bensonhurst, so we spoke the same language. We ran into him at a couple of fights. It wasn't like all the guys would call him up and say, "We're going out to dinner and we want you along," but if we were out to dinner and he came over to the table, everyone would say hi. If Sid was on *The Sopranos* I don't know if you'd need to whack him; he needs more of a slap. I hope he doesn't fuck up anymore.

Hey, At Least It Wasn't Me This Time

I was on the air that day: April 4, 2007. I was doing the show from Florida. I had called into *Imus*, something I had been doing quite frequently during that stretch. Even though Chris Carlin was there doing sports, I still called in. When the Rutgers thing went down, I honestly didn't think much of it.

I reported on the Rutgers-Tennessee NCAA women's final from the night before. Bernard McGuirk said the Rutgers team looked like "hard-core hos." Then Imus added "Nappy-headed hos." Then I said, "The more I look at Rutgers, they look exactly like the Toronto Raptors." Listen, comparing women's basketball players to men's basketball players, whether it's the WNBA or college basketball, has been going on forever. They look like men, some of them. It's just a fact. I can't think of anything less attractive than a woman dunking a basketball, but that's just me.

The show was on a Wednesday. The media frenzy didn't start to pick up steam until Friday, but it was a maelstrom. Imus was very apologetic, and I thought he was sincere in everything he did, from going to talk to the girls and making apologies. The comment cost him his job. Thank God he's back and doing great. He certainly had to suffer through a lot, losing his job and being publicly humiliated. At the end of the day I also believe if that crazed gunmen at Virginia Tech had done what he'd done a week earlier, then Imus would still be working at CBS. There's no doubt in my mind. It was a slow week, newswise. Media Matters and a couple of these Internet sites got a hold of the Imus story, and of course it got to Al Sharpton. And the rest is history.

Looking back, it was probably an unfortunate comment. But I also think it's unfair that radio people get labeled so quickly. If you make a passing joke or two, even if it's offensive, people are quick to put a name on it. I've done that—I've said offensive things, I've said hurtful things, I've said irresponsible things. But when you're on the air for four, five hours a day, every single day that can happen. Making a joke doesn't make a person hateful or racist or misogynist.

Unfortunately, all you have to do is say one thing these days, and between the Internet and the media, you've got your label. I think that's unfair.

At the end of the day, I don't think he should have been fired. I think he got railroaded. I really do. It was the sponsors. The radio business is like every other business—it's still about money. Of course, I wasn't told what was going on, but I think his dismissal was more about money, the possibility of losing sponsors. There are two M-words, *morality* and *money*, and I think that money speaks louder.

I don't want to speak for Mark Chernoff or Imus, but it was my sense that things were going really well with us. I felt that if they had continued to go smoothly, I would have been back—certainly on the *Imus* show but also back at the FAN doing some other things as well. I think it is very, very likely that by September 2007 I would have been back at FAN full time. There's no doubt the Rutgers thing absolutely derailed me. I was doing a really good job. Imus was bringing me on more and more. Unfortunately, it was not to be.

WE NOW INTERRUPT OUR REGULARLY SCHEDULED BROADCAST FOR A WORD FROM...

CHRIS CARLIN, SNY Mets on-air host, former WFAN personality

I had heard about Sid. I didn't know him at all, not from a hole in the wall. It was the Super Bowl in Miami in January 1999, Denver and the Falcons, Radio Row. I was in this hotel lobby. I'm producing *Mike and the Mad Dog* on FAN, and this goofy-looking dude comes over to me and just starts screaming "Continent, how are ya, baby!" and he just comes up and hugs me, out of nowhere. He goes, "I'm Sid." We talk for a minute, he's kissing Mike Francesa's ass, kissing Chris Russo's ass, the whole thing. And then he says to me, "Here, here's two tickets to Dennis Rodman's party tonight. I'll see you there. It will be great!" So he hands me these two tickets. I can't go, I had plans that night, so I gave them to a buddy of mine. They weren't tickets so much as they looked like the strip club ads that are handed out on the street. It turns out they were just about as good. My buddy goes to the door of the party, and they look at him like he has four heads. To me, that's Sid. The promise is always better than the payoff.

Sid is a complex figure for me. I like him, but I also hate him. I like him because genuinely, deep down, under every aspect of being an idiot, Sid actually has a good heart somewhere, but it doesn't always come out. Look, Sid's funny. Say what you will about Sid, he can definitely be funny and very quick. I had a chance to do a couple of shows with him a few years back, and I really enjoyed doing it. I think he is infinitely more talented than many people who are on the radio right now. I'm not going to say he's more talented than Mike Francesa, but there are a lot of guys right now who have shows that Sid's absolutely better than, no question.

At the same time, Sid will step on anyone or anything to get whatever he wants, and he has no qualms about it. Sid on multiple occasions got fired from different gigs, whether it was the Giants pregame or *Imus*, and for the years following that I'd step into his former roles. He did everything he possibly could to get the job back, to get me out of the way. He could not care less about anything to do with me.

Sid was a much better fit for the *Imus* show than I ever was. It didn't help him being on *Imus*, insofar as avoiding saying something stupid. You want to take the ultimate incident, Sid was there filling in for me on the morning Imus said what he said about the Rutgers women's basketball team because I was out sick. Do I think that if I was there it would have been different? I think it's possible. Imus knew I had a relationship with Rutgers and he might not have gone down that road, but I absolutely believe Sid was involved in that conversation. I don't want to use the word "instigator," but there's no question that whole atmosphere was fostered by his presence. Sid said something along the lines of the Rutgers team reminded him of the Toronto Raptors. You're just shaking your head listening to it like, *Oh, God.* Sid, being there, pushed that even a little bit further. The day before, I was feeling sick during the show. I got violently ill, just the worst stomach flu you can imagine possible. It carried into the next day, and that was when the Rutgers thing with Imus happened. Do I think it was the best-timed stomach flu I've ever had? Yes. Or ever will have? Yes.

I don't know that Sid is capable of doing the right thing. I wouldn't trust him with anything value of mine, and Sid's one of the few guys I know who would hear that comment and say, "Yeah, that's probably about right. I wouldn't trust me either." I'm actually not speaking ill of him when I say that. He's a good talk show host, if he just wasn't stupid in so many ways. And I say that lovingly, I really do.

WE NOW INTERRUPT OUR REGULARLY SCHEDULED BROADCAST
FOR A WORD FROM...

RICHARD "BO" DIETL,
Former New York City police detective

I worked with Sid on the *Imus* show for several years. After 9/11 we did something together. He was talking about going to the cleaners and picking up the wrong shirts, like six or seven shirts. He brought them home and he says, "They gave me the wrong shirts, but they were nice shirts so I wore 'em anyway." We put together this whole skit. He was the only one who didn't know about it. We had some guy call up and say, "You know, those shirts were from one of the people that got killed over in the World Trade Center. Those were my brother's shirts. You have my brother's shirts. I'm going to come and get you." We kind of set him up. I brought a guy named Johnny C. in who is an actual stunt man and a six-degree black belt, a tough guy. We made him be the brother. We brought him on the show, and he was questioning Sid, "How could you take my brother's shirts? That's pretty screwed up. You take somebody's shirts who died in the World Trade Center and you wear them? What kind of an animal are you?"

It really progressed, and all of a sudden Johnny went like crazy. That was part of the act. He actually picked up a computer and threw it at Sid. Sid ran out of the studio screaming and was hiding in Imus' back office. He's saying, "Bo, you have to help me. Call the police! Call the police!" I told him, "Don't worry. I'll take care of it." He was in the back office shitting in his pants, it was so funny. All of a sudden we brought him back in the studio and told him it was all a setup.

Sometimes they got a little nervous with Sid because he goes a little over the top. I was in the studio when he said the Venus Williams–Serena Williams remark. He said they shouldn't have been on the cover of *Playboy*, they should be on the cover of *National Geographic*. You know, over the years we've said so much stuff. People listen to it and they zero in on what they want to zero in on. He said it in a joking manner, and you know what? If it wasn't a stupid environment that we're in, it would have been just laughed upon and that would have been the end of it.

I mean, I've said stuff on the air. When Patrick Ewing was with the Knicks, I was in a restaurant, and Ewing was there. He wouldn't sign my friend's son's autograph, so I talked about him on the air. I said, "When those lights go on before the game, you see Ewing coming in there, and his arms are so long he's got roller skates on his knuckles because they're dragging on the floor." Stuff like that would be considered funny, but in today's day and age they'll call you a racist for saying something like that.

Sid must go over the top. He doesn't know where the line is, so that's a problem. I think he's a very talented person, fast talking, a fast wit. He is able to have that stuff come out pretty quickly. He always played it on the edge. That was the ongoing joke: What was Sid going to say to get thrown off again?

WE NOW INTERRUPT OUR REGULARLY SCHEDULED BROADCAST
FOR A WORD FROM...

JOE BENIGNO, WFAN host

I knew Sid a little bit from being on the Imus show and from doing the 10:00–1:00 before I did. He was doing it with Jody McDonald. I started at FAN in '95. I was there a while before Sid ever got there. I was doing overnights. Actually, I did wonder why he got the 10:00–1:00 job before me. I really didn't know him at that point, and I did wonder, *Who is this guy coming in? I've been here six or seven years doing overnights. This guy's doing 10:00–1:00? What's that all about?* I knew he was funny on *Imus*, that's fine, but why should he be doing that? He got that ridiculously quickly.

He made a comment that actually ticked me off at one point. I still really didn't know him. He compared me in some way to Osama Bin Laden when he was on *Imus*. He said something to the effect that I would fly a plane into a building, something involving the Jets. That pissed me off. It wasn't that long after 9/11. What are you doing? You're comparing me to Osama Bin Laden, a fucking terrorist? It did bother me, and I talked to Sid about it and we straightened it out. That's before I really got to know him.

I thought he was great on *Imus*. He was a good talk show host, he's very entertaining, and he definitely knows his sports. I always felt on *Imus* he was just tremendous because he would really go over the top. He had to control himself a little bit on the 10:00–1:00 show. Sid would basically do anything for a laugh. I was never offended by what Sid said. You know the deal. The political correctness in this country is out of control to begin with, as far as I'm concerned. I always felt he was just doing what Imus wanted him to do. It was what Imus wanted him to be, and he did it brilliantly.

Sid and I started to get a little friendly. We had a couple of crazy nights out. We both were represented by Mark Lepselter, and we kind of always talked about it: Sid wanted me with him and I wanted to be with him too, not only because I wanted to get off overnights but to be able to work with him as well.

I will say this—maybe it's because of the stuff I do on television and me being more comfortable with myself than I've ever been—I do kind of think I've gone much more toward being an entertainer than just a talk show host. Being the kind of guy I am, I think I'm a pretty cool dude. I'm basically up for anything. I'm not as crazy and over the top as Sid and not self-destructive like Sid, but there are areas that Sid would go through I would go through too. I'm not going to do something that's going to eventually kill me.

One night we went out because one of the girls working on *Imus* was leaving. It was a party for her, a bunch of people from the FAN went, and then we went to this after-hours place. Sid has some coke. I hadn't done it in a while. I've done it in my life—I'm not going to say I hadn't done it—but not in a long time, years at that point. We're in the bathroom of this freaking place, and Sid's trying to get me into the freaking stall. He pulls me into the fucking bathroom stall ready to do this coke, and I'm saying "Sid, what the fuck are you doing?" Can you imagine this? I say, "Me and you, two fucking guys, WFAN talk show hosts, caught in the bathroom snorting cocaine? Are you out of your mind?"

We weren't together that long. We started together in November 2004. At that point I'd done a little over nine years of overnights when I got the shot. I worked with him until February 2005 when he ended up going into rehab. That was a trip, too. The night before he went into rehab was like the last show we would do together for almost two months. Sid came back in April or May of that year, and then we did the show together from May only until September '05. It was opening day of the 2005 football season, Herman Edwards' last year with the Jets. The day Sid got fired, the Jets got killed by Kansas City. It was a disaster on their way to that 4–12 shit last year of Herman. I was not even with Sid for a year.

I thought we did a good show together, especially if they let us go places where they wouldn't let the 10:00–1:00 show go before. I was all for bringing more entertainment people into it. I was all for doing more with girls. They let us go that way a little bit. They gave us a little more leeway than maybe normally they would give to that show, but not as much we wanted. Sid was always fighting that with them. I was all for it. I would take it to a certain level; I'm all for bringing girls in and chatting with them. I have no problem with that. They didn't want us to go there too much.

I loved being his partner. It was great. I would just kind of play off Sid, let him do his thing and react to that. It was easy. After nine years of being with myself on the overnights with very few commercials and all of that, I was in a situation where I was doing three hours. It was a different dynamic, and I loved working with him. It's too bad, because if he would have been around now I think we would have really…. Well, Evan Roberts and I have done a tremendous job, our ratings are great, and I love working with Evan, but Sid and I would have had a really different kind of 10:00–1:00 show. I think they eventually would have let us really go more into adding in the entertainment quality as well as the sports as time went on. And I think we really would have had a tremendous show. We'll never know.

His foibles got in the way of the show because he went into rehab. I was upset when I found out that day. I found out he was in rehab, but I knew he was coming back. When he was fired on the Giants' opening day, I was stunned. It was devastating a little bit. It was rough day. I get this news, and there I was, on the opening Sunday of the 2005 football season, a brand new year. To me, there's nothing better than football. Maybe girls. I got a phone call at about 11:00 AM from Lep. He lets me know what's happening, says, "It's over. It's done. They fired him," and tells me the whole story. It put an immediate damper on the whole day. And then of course the Jets just made it even better. They get their fucking asses kicked, and the Chiefs ran for about 320 yards that day between Priest Holmes and Larry Johnson. And that was it. I was by myself for more than a year until Evan came along.

Messier: Now There's a Guy Whose Word Is Bond

I did not grow up in a household in which hockey was a big deal. My dad was always a die-hard baseball fan. He grew up in a Brooklyn Dodgers family, and he's been a Mets fan since they first came on the scene. He's always been a die-hard Giants football fan. But hockey and basketball were not big in my house. Those I acquired on my own and much later in life.

I started to follow the Rangers in the late 1970s. I was attending Poly Prep in Brooklyn, and there would always be fights—Mets vs. Yankees, Giants vs. Jets, Phil Simms or Richard Todd, that type of nonsense. Ranger-Islander fights were great and I wanted to join the fray. We literally had fistfights in the halls arguing about Ron Duguay vs. Mike Bossy, Bryan Trottier, Butch Goring, Clark Gillies, and all those great teams.

So I started watching the Rangers. Ron Duguay was always my favorite Rangers player. They lost in 1979 to the Canadiens and John Davidson was the goaltender, but I really became interested right after that. Some of those epic battles in the playoffs between the Rangers and the Islanders (of course the Islanders would always win. They won four Stanley Cups) were epic. Those Rangers teams, when they had Duguay, Ron Greschner, Mark Pavelich, and Eddie Mio took over in the nets, those were the best. Mio was a guy I really liked. When I went down to Florida to college in 1985, my fandom for the Rangers kind of waned. By the time I got married in 1992, the Rangers got Mark Messier. And that's when the Rangers became a big deal for me again.

It's a really special thing that New York has. Everybody knows that New York is a baseball town. It's more about the Yankees and the Mets than it is about the Giants and the Jets. But the beauty about the Rangers is they're kind of New York. Other markets have their football teams and their baseball teams, but the Rangers are so much a part of the fabric in this city. You're talking about Madison Square Garden and the Mecca that it is. You're talking about midtown Manhattan. And the Rangers are one of the Original Six hockey teams. To me, they're a New York treasure.

Hockey is a niche sport. It doesn't have nearly the degree of popularity that baseball, football, and basketball have, but the fans are loyal and rabid, and they don't go anywhere. Ranger fans don't flip-flop.

The Rangers' championship in 1994 is still my favorite championship of all time—more than the Giants' two Super Bowls, more than being there for the ticker tape parade in 1986 when the Mets won the World Series. (I've not celebrated a Knicks championship because I was six years old in 1973, the last time they did it.)

Messier was everybody's favorite, obviously. It's funny, because when you talk about the great New York players in my generation—Derek Jeter, Patrick Ewing, Phil Simms and Lawrence Taylor, Darryl Strawberry and Dwight Gooden—what do they all have in common? For the most part, they spent their time with one team, and they starred for that team. I can't think of another athlete besides Messier who in the history of New York lore had his better days someplace else. You can't compare what Mark Messier accomplished with the Rangers with what he did in Edmonton with the Oilers. The guy won five Cups there. It was the greatest team of all time. The guy skated with Wayne Gretzky. But the fact was that the Rangers had not won a cup in 50 years and that

Rangers fans, as die-hard and rabid as any hockey fans in the world of one of the great hockey organizations in the world had waited 50 years to win a Stanley Cup made it special. When they got a guy in Messier who is one of the greatest players of all time, it was easy to start feeling like, *Hey, we can win this thing.*

And then of course he went out there in that Devils series, the game before the Matteau game. The Rangers were down 3–2 and won Game 6 on a night when Mark Messier had an even-strength hat trick. He guaranteed a win. How many times has Patrick Ewing guaranteed a win and the finger-roll rolled out? The only guy who guaranteed a win and got it was Namath in 1969. Mark Messier strolls into town, with the Rangers facing elimination at the hands of the Devils, and says, "We're definitely going to win." Not only do the Rangers win that game, but he gets a fucking hat trick! It was one of the greatest moments in the history of New York sports! Messier had spent the majority of his monster seasons in Edmonton, but the fact that he delivered a Stanley Cup to New York for the first time in 50 years, the fact that he guaranteed a victory, got the victory, and got the hat trick—all that is such an incredible story. Who else has done something like that? Ewing was always a Knick (I don't even count his short time in Seattle). L.T. was always a Giant. Jeter always a Yankee. I can't think of another New York player who gets the love and admiration that Mark Messier gets when, truth be told, his best days by far were spent elsewhere. Sure, Gary Carter was an Expo, and Keith Hernandez won a World Series in St. Louis before winning one with the Mets. But Messier was the face of the organization. It was his team, and he delivered that Stanley Cup.

When the Rangers got Wayne Gretzky, that was exciting. For a couple of years, Gretzky and Messier had a chance to get back to the Cup together. They lost to Eric Lindros and the Flyers in the Eastern Conference Finals, and that was it. Gretzky hung around for a couple of years, but Messier signed that big deal in Vancouver.

I was at Madison Square Garden on the night when, after those couple of years in Vancouver, Messier came back to the Rangers. It was his first night back at Madison Square Garden, and that place was just crazy. Of course they didn't win any Cups after that and in fact have had very little playoff success, outside of Jaromir Jagr a few years ago.

The GM, Neil Smith, was the guy who took a beating. After the Rangers won the Cup and Gretzky and Messier were gone, he went out there and tried to acquire all these Western Conference players—guys like Theo Fleury and Valeri Kamensky. He got all these flashy West Coast players who just didn't play well inside the East Coast, where the Devils play the trap defense, and it's a lot more difficult. Smith got fired because he spent lots and lots of money on guys who couldn't get it done in New York. Then they brought in Glenn Sather, and he has spent all kinds of money to bring in players who have done nothing. At least Neil Smith was there when they won the Cup.

Glenn Sather has done nothing. Everybody kills James Dolan for holding onto Isiah Thomas for too long. Sure, Sather has had a little more success than Thomas did, but the fact remains that the Rangers have not been very good. They make it to the playoffs every once in a while, but they don't have a lot of success. Sather enjoyed all that success in Edmonton, but that was a long time ago. I maintain that if you gave me Mark Messier, Wayne Gretzky, Jari Kurri, Glenn Anderson, Paul Coffey, Grant Fuhr, Jeff Beukeboom, Kevin Lowe, Esa Tikkanen, and Craig MacTavish, I could probably win a couple of Stanley Cups, too. He came to New York based on his success in Edmonton years and years ago, when he had the best roster in the history of the game, and since then he's done shit. And he still commands a huge salary! Just as Dolan was ridiculously loyal to Isiah, he has been to Sather. Sather should be gone. To me it's about the personnel on this hockey team, and Sather has not done a very good job. I've had enough.

If You're on This List, You Already Know That I Hate Your Guts

I readily admitted in the press that there have been things that I have said over the years that I would take back. Of course there have been. But I've never considered myself a vicious person, nor has anybody who knows me. In fact, I'm one of the nicest people you'll ever meet. I'm a good family guy. But I've said some things in an effort to be controversial and funny that I shouldn't have said. I always warn people that radio provides that opportunity in those couple of seconds. I once talked about this with Mike Francesa. He was doing sports on *Imus* years ago when he first started at FAN. He said that Imus was very tough on him, and there were days—though he never said anything as crazy as I did, obviously—when he felt undue pressure to be crazier than usual. I'm not blaming Don Imus, but to judge a person for what they say in a fleeting comment on the radio is stupid. It's equally as irresponsible as the person saying it. If you get to know me and don't like me, that's fine. If someone thinks I'm horrible on the air, I'm okay with that. But to say, "Sid's a lowlife" because I made a stupid, irresponsible, offensive, and quite frankly hurtful comment, is unfair. I paid the price. I was humiliated. I was in every paper. I was fired. But for people to think that that comment was indicative of my beliefs is unfair.

Imus brought me back. It turns out Imus has been through a lot of shit in his career as well, and at the end of the day he's kind of forgiving. I talked to Howard Stern about it, too. Obviously Howard doesn't give a shit. He says horrible things about everybody. He felt the same way. It's the First Amendment. It's freedom of speech.

I once called NBC's David Gregory a douchebag, so he's no fan of mine, not that he ever was. I said, "They should change the name of the show he does from *Meet the Press* to *Meet the Putz*. Is there a bigger douchebag on all of TV than David Gregory, outside of Nancy Grace?" It was my responsibility to watch the Sunday morning news shows for Imus, so I watched Bob Schieffer and Chris Wallace and Chris Matthews and George Stephanopoulos—and of course David Gregory, who turned out to be the biggest backstabbing son of a bitch of everybody. He, Keith Olbermann, and all those guys at NBC used to come on *Imus* and promote their shows all the time. As soon as the Rutgers thing happened, they all ran away from Imus and went behind his back, telling the bosses that he should be fired. Gregory was on almost every day as the chief White House correspondent. He was funny, and Imus would pump him up. As soon as the shit went down with Imus, he fucking turned his back on him. It's ironic that both Imus and I have great relationships with Chuck Todd, who is the NBC White House correspondent now.

* * *

Nancy Grace, who used to be on Court TV and now is on CNN, is someone that I had a memorable moment with on *Imus in the Morning*. I don't like Nancy Grace. That said, I watch her show almost every night. She has stories on that I care about. Kids disappear, and she's all over those stories. She has become the harbinger for missing kids across the country. I'm moved and intrigued by them, so I watch the show. But I can't stand her—the way she treats the defense attorneys. She treats everyone as guilty, no matter what. Maybe it's because she was a prosecutor. She has also been through a real-life tragedy: she was engaged to a guy in college who was murdered. She has since married and has twin kids and a nice life, but she still has a hard-on for the world. She brings on these defense attorneys, guys like Mickey Sherman, and just fucking humiliates them. I can't stand watching it. She's nasty.

Years ago, when the whole Kobe Bryant thing went down, most people thought Kobe Bryant was guilty. Ballplayers, athletes, you hear about them with women all the time. I think most people think they're guilty, outside of the sycophant fans. I always thought Nancy Grace had a little bit more of a responsibility to play it down the middle because she is on TV. She has to stick to the facts rather then just say, "Fuck him, he's a ballplayer." I was killing her on Imus' show: "This Nancy Grace, she's got Kobe guilty before all the facts are in." I made the analogy that Nancy Grace, to me, is a lot like the matter they found in the girl's underwear in Colorado after Kobe left her hotel room that night. It was kind of a nasty thing to say.

So of course Imus brought on Nancy Grace. I'm in the studio with Imus and, like he does with everybody else, he always finds a way to say, "Hey, by the way, Sid Rosenberg doesn't like you." He brought up the whole story right there on the spot. I think Imus' intention was to get something brewing, because I don't think he really likes Nancy Grace either. I don't think anybody likes Nancy Grace. She refused to go back and forth with him. She just said something like, her father told her a long time ago, when you go to bed with a dog you wake up with fleas. And that was it.

* * *

Jeff Greenfield is the one guy I never got along with. He's a stuffed shirt. I had just done my sports report on *Imus*, and he came on moments later. He was going on and on about his son, who was 12 years old at the time. He said to Imus, "Oh, my son knows so much about baseball and sports. I could easily see him one day doing what Sid does or doing what Breen does, being a sports guy." I came on right afterward. I was kind of being sarcastic and joking around—I didn't mean to be nasty to Jeff Greenfield. I don't even know the guy or his kid. But I was so sick and tired of hearing it. All parents think his or her kid knows more about sports than every other kid. And by the way, even if your dumb kid knows about sports, it doesn't mean he's ever going to be a successful radio guy. It takes a little more than knowing about sports. You have to be funny and spontaneous, and you have to deliver it in the right fashion. So I said as much. I think Greenfield got very, very angry that day.

Two or three shows before FAN and NBC canceled *Imus*, it was already out there that he was in big trouble and that he could be suspended or fired. The people who came on were all sort of saying their goodbyes. I think they saw the writing on the wall. Some people were coming on giving their opinion as to why or why not he shouldn't be fired. Greenfield came on and said, "Look, I-man, I've been coming on for 20 or 30 years, and I'm a huge fan or yours and the show, but you have to be careful. It's one thing when you have Mike Breen come on and do sports, but it's another when you have a guy like Sid Rosenberg."

I was on my bed watching the show on MSNBC when he said it. It came out of nowhere. *Breen is funny and safe, and then they bring on Sid and all these controversies have popped up and it's not good for you, I-Man.* That's basically what he was saying. He said that two or three days before Imus lost his job with NBC and FAN, and I haven't forgotten it. I've called him a douchebag a couple of times on the Imus show.

* * *

I'm in my early forties and I watch a lot of TV. I consider myself a TV junkie. I watch everything from the sporting events to the news shows. I'll watch a little bit of whatever's on CNN, whatever's on CNBC. I'm a huge MSNBC fan, but I think Keith Olbermann is a backstabbing son of a bitch. He's brilliant, and he's great on TV. He was good on ESPN and he's even better on *Countdown*, but he's a spineless, backstabbing piece of shit. I know for a fact that he went to the higher-ups at NBC and made sure Imus got canned, even though Imus was always a defender of his. Sure, he would take shots at Keith as well, as he does with everyone, but he certainly went above and beyond to try to promote Olbermann's show in his early days at MSNBC. And all Keith did was shit all over Imus when it came time for Imus' reckoning. I was part of that Imus crew, so I never forgot that. Guys like Olbermann and Spike Lee coming after me, guys like Jesse Jackson—those guys can all go fuck themselves.

* * *

Mike and Mike in the Morning on ESPN Radio? I like Mike Greenberg. Greenie's pretty good, but I think Mike Golic sucks. I think he's the stereotypical former athlete. He thinks he knows everything because he played a couple of years in the NFL, but he doesn't know dick. I'm not a big fan of any of those shows. Colin Cowherd knows his sports, but the fact that this guy is on a billion stations across the country and does television for ESPN is mind-boggling. What's so fucking great about Colin Cowherd? For years, I never liked Dan Patrick. I thought he was kind of dull and boring on the air, and then I started listening on a regular basis and then he and I developed a relationship. He would actually come on my show down in Florida quite a bit. And now I admit I'm a big fan of his show.

I think Jim Rome sucks. Okay, I shouldn't say he sucks, but I don't get it. He makes a fucking fortune! He's a California guy and he's got his own lingo. When I hear him on the East Coast, I just don't get it. He gets great guests and he's plugged in; there's no doubt about it. He's a legitimate star in the business—and all because he fucking called Jim Everett "Chris Everett." Listen, he's a smart guy. I can't knock him. He's done well for himself. But he's not my cup of tea. I'm an East Coast guy, and he's got that West Coast bullshit lingo that just annoys the hell out of me. I'm a Brooklyn guy. I don't get that garbage.

I listen to all these guys and some of them are making tons of money and I just don't know why. I like JT the Brick, but the rest of Fox Sports Radio is no good. I give all these guys credit—Mike and Mike and Colin Cowherd—all of these guys that have taken their shows to 100 different cities and are doing well financially. But at the end of the day I don't know why they make so much money or why they're revered. Quite frankly, I don't think any of them are as good as I am. That might come off arrogant and obnoxious and they might think, *Fuck Sid*, but I'm telling you, none of them are as good as I am.

The problem is that I've been labeled a certain way, which is a bunch of bullshit. Some of these opportunities just don't come my way because some of the executives in this business are a bunch of pussies. There was a time when people cared about putting on good radio. That's what is important to me; I want to put on a good show. In this age, in this economic climate, most guys just want to collect a couple hundred thousand dollars, show up to work, and not have any problems.

There was a time you could lose an advertiser or two and still make it in radio. Now you lose one advertiser, and they want to fire you. These fucking guys who wear their suit and tie every day don't know dick about radio. All they're about is the bottom line. To them, controversy isn't worth it. It's not worth putting on something great or something different because, God forbid, if something happens that affects the show financially, they're going to lose their jobs. I understand the rationale, but the fact is, they're pussies. Nobody wants to take chances any more. Nobody cares about great radio anymore. Those days are over, man.

What's the Big Idea About Steroids, Anyway?

I don't care about steroids at all. I couldn't care less. One of my favorite players of all time is Mike Piazza, and I'm convinced he was on steroids. I am resigned to the fact that there was a whole era of it. Let me ask you this: why should I care about it if Major League Baseball didn't care about it? All these investigations and the nonsense going on right now seems very, very convenient, but when this stuff first came to baseball's attention—way before José Canseco's books and all that nonsense and even before the summer of Mark McGwire and Sammy Sosa—Major League Baseball knew about it and turned a blind eye.

If not for that summer of 1998 when McGwire and Sosa chased that home run record, baseball could be dead right now. Bud Selig knew what was going on. He also knew that summer saved baseball. If baseball didn't give a shit and baseball loved the fact that Brady Anderson went from 16 home runs to 50 in one year, why should I give a shit? It's not as if the playing field wasn't equal. It's not as if certain teams couldn't use steroids. They were available to everybody. If your guys used them, great; if your guys didn't, your loss. It's not like they said, "McGwire and Canseco can do it in Oakland, but Piazza can't do it in New York." It was available to everybody, and all the big players did it.

175

Think about it, outside of Albert Pujols, in the last 10, 15 years—whether it's been Bonds, McGwire, Sosa, Rafael Palmeiro, A-Rod, Manny Ramirez, Piazza—who *hasn't* used them? Maybe Ken Griffey Jr. and Pujols. Steroids were easy to get, and baseball wasn't going to bother anybody about it—until of course it became a full-blown epidemic and José Canseco alerted the world about it. That was ironic, because I was the only guy at WFAN who believed José Canseco. Mike, Chris, Benigno, everybody else said, "He's a clown. He's got a hard-on for baseball. Don't listen to him." But I believed him and I brought him and his wife on the air. For years and years baseball had turned a blind eye. Why should I be mad as a fan?

Show me a guy who's beating his wife—I can't root for that guy. Show me a guy who committed a heinous crime—I can't root for that guy. But if there's a guy out there trying to get a competitive advantage in the world of sports, is it cheating? Sure, if you want to put an asterisk next to his name, I'm okay with that. If you want to keep him out of the Hall of Fame, fine—just make sure you keep them all out. I think it's ridiculous. I think Barry Bonds should be in the Hall of Fame because Bonds was a three-time MVP with the Pirates when he was a stick figure. Some of those guys put up some great numbers before they were on the juice. Unfortunately, we don't have the exact numbers. We can't say, "Well, he hit 400 home runs before and 200 after." For me, if you leave them all out of the Hall of Fame, I'm okay with that, and if you put them all in I'm okay with that. Personally, I think they all belong there.

At this point, nobody will surprise me. Even if Griffey and Pujols admitted to using them, it wouldn't surprise me. Once A-Rod went down, that was it. Derek Jeter would surprise me, but he has never hit more than 20-something home runs in a year. It's one thing for Bonds and McGwire and Griffey and A-Rod—guys who will hit 500, 600, 700 home runs in their career. Jeter would be the one player who would shock the baseball world and maybe even rock baseball just a little. He's such a deity in Major League Baseball, and he stands for everything good.

For all the yelling and screaming that happens on sports talk radio, if you look at the numbers—attendance, merchandising, the MLB package—the sport is healthier than ever. That's a fact. Of course it angers me when Roger Clemens stands up and denies using. But it's no different than Bill Clinton getting up there and saying, "I did not have sex with that woman." It's human nature. I've been put in that position, where somebody said, "You did this," and I denied it. What do you expect human beings to do, say, "You're right. You got me." There's a lot at stake for Roger Clemens: the Hall of Fame, his reputation. I think he's going to deny it until he goes to prison if he has to for committing perjury.

I wasn't surprised Clemens did it. But it didn't make me feel any worse about him. I thought he was a scumbag before that. He didn't have me fooled. Anybody that had a lot of success over that period of time (outside of two or three guys) was on the juice.

I think there are human growth hormones out there now. I'm convinced that the people out there are one step ahead of baseball. Whether you have to lather yourself up with HGH and rub it from your head to your penis to your toes or whatever you can do, I believe that professional athletes will always do whatever they can to get the competitive advantage and get the big-money contracts. They will always be one step ahead of tests. Are they doing anabolic steroids right now or putting needles into their asses? Probably not, but they're doing something, I'll tell you that. There is something out there that we haven't figured out how to test for that gives these guys a competitive advantage. I'm convinced of that. There will be another scandal. HGH maybe, who knows? But come up with a couple of letters, and that will be your next scandal.

Florida, Where I Found Southern Comfort (the Other Kind)

When the WFAN thing fell apart in 2005, where was I going to go? Right back to Florida. I had been talking to the guys at 790 in Miami before I left New York. They were putting together a start-up station, and the producer said, "Come to Miami. The weather's great, and we'll pay you a lot of money. Why do you want to play second fiddle to Imus and Mike and the Mad Dog?" After I was fired, I'd lost all my leverage. It was one thing to talk to them when I was working at the FAN and thinking about relocating. It was another thing when I was out of a job. But I still had my family, and for that I was always very fortunate.

Months before I left the FAN, I came to the feeling that I was never going to be higher than No. 4 there. It was always going to be Imus, Mike, and Chris. I wasn't happy being No. 4, even though I understood it. I respected it, but that didn't mean I was okay with it. My ego told me that I am every bit as good as Imus, Mike, or Chris. Why should I have to settle for No. 4? The same thought rolled around in my head, *Is it better to be a medium-sized fish in a huge pond or a huge fish in a small pond?* I wanted my show at FAN to be part Imus, part *Mike and the Mad Dog*, and part Stern—and it was never going to be that. I was fighting with the program director, Eric Spitz, all the time. He didn't have the power to fuck with Imus—Imus wouldn't even let Spitz into his office. Spitz wasn't going to fuck with Mike and the Mad Dog, either. So the only show Spitz really had any power over (even though as the program director you're supposed to have power over everybody) was the show that Benigno and I had. All of a sudden, at 10:00 AM I became Eric Spitz's whipping boy. It was a constant battle.

I came down to Florida in September 2005, and by November I was back on the air at 790 The Ticket. They paired me with O.J. McDuffie. Their biggest reason was that he's a local guy and people love him. They wanted to make sure the transition for me, a New Yorker coming down to Miami, didn't have such a rough landing. The thought was that if I started talking about the Giants, at least O.J., the great, legendary Miami Dolphin, would be there to smooth it over.

I was at 790 from November 2005 through March 2009. There are a lot of New Yorkers down in Florida. It's great. As soon as they heard my voice it was like, *Oh my God, I'm home.* I really believe that. It's a weird place. People think Florida is New York with palm trees—and that's true until you get south of Fort Lauderdale. When you start getting to Kendall and Homestead and parts of Miami, those are the people who don't appreciate the New Yorkers. The old Cuban population that has been there forever and the really entrenched Miami people, they actually can't stand the snowbirds from New York. They feel as if we come down here and take shit over and that we're always talking about how great New York is. If you come down here and go to Fort Lauderdale, South Beach, or Boca Raton, you feel like it's like New York. But once you get into Dade County, it's different. It's a geographical bias that I have to deal with every single day. My listeners hear my accent, and right away I become the enemy.

The fans down in Miami are not nearly as passionate—or, for that matter, as intelligent—as New York fans. I don't want to call my fan base stupid, but it's not the same. There still are a lot of people who are transplants. The real Dolphins fans never hooked on with the Heat or the Panthers. Those latter fans are younger. They're set in their ways and they're small in numbers compared to the passionate sports fans up in New York. They're passionate about the Dolphins and they're passionate about the Hurricanes, and everything else they can take or leave. You can talk baseball for four hours in February in New York. During the baseball season, I'll be lucky to take four baseball phone calls in Florida. It's a big difference.

We had philosophical differences along the way at 790. They want the show to be more locally oriented; they would have been happy if I talked about the Heat, the Panthers, and the Marlins all day, every day. That was never going to happen. They wanted a guy who was looking to be entrenched, not a guy who was looking to be on *Imus* up in New York, who wanted to do *The Howard Stern Show*. You want my real opinion? They didn't want to pay me. The shit hit the fan, the economy tanked, and in November 2008 all of a sudden they were starting to complain about things they never complained about before, some of the stuff I was doing on the side in New York. I had two-plus years left on my contract, I was making good money, and I believe they wanted to get out of that. In this day and age contracts are not what they used to be. You can easily get out of a contract—especially with a guy like me who's had a checkered, controversial past. There was no big reason why I left. I wasn't caught drunk or high nor did I miss work for a week. But I was gone all the same. I was out of work for six months because of my noncompete clause. It was a very difficult time. Money was obviously a situation for me and Danielle.

I met Joe Bell, the GM of WQAM not long after I got down to Florida. While I was at 790, my contract stated very specifically that we could not talk. I saw Bell at the diner every once in a while, because the stations are right across the street from each other. Every time I saw him he was great, friendly. It was obvious to me he was a fan. It wasn't long after my gig ended at 790 that Joe Bell and I contacted each other.

QAM has been around forever. It's kind of like the Miami equivalent of the FAN. The Ticket came on the scene a couple of years ago, which makes it more of a corollary to 1050 ESPN in New York. The only difference is 1050 still gets murdered by FAN. No one even takes 1050 seriously, even now. Down in Miami, 790 was winning for a while. Now QAM has the edge. The two most important teams in this town, the Dolphins and the Hurricanes, are with QAM. The station has been here forever, and it has the better reputation. We came along at 790 as these young gunslingers and tough guys, and we made our mark very quickly. Now, Joe Rose and I, two of the biggest talents in this town, are at QAM.

I love my show. I believe it will be the best show I've ever done. I've been promised by the powers that be that I'll be allowed to do *my* show. If the ratings come back and they're horrendous, then yes, I'll change. I'll work in Timbuktu. I'll quit the fucking business. I'm not trying to sound like a tough guy, but I'd quit the business before I do a show that somebody else wants me to do. Am I willing to tweak my show if the ratings aren't great? Of course. I have a certain philosophy that Mad Dog hated and I love. My philosophy is, you have to put it all in there. It's all planned. I'm the only guy in this business that I know of who picks every single song coming back from break. That's how neurotic I am. My show has a certain sound. I'm the fast-talking guy, the guy who loves to go to Vegas, the guy who gambled on football and did a lot of drugs in the '80s. I always talk about the '80s—the movies, music, women, and drugs. To me the '80s were the best decade ever.

The same guys who want to talk about Dolphins football also like movies and music. I'm a part of the 25 to 54 demographic, and I believe that guys in that age group like music, they like movies, they like TV, and they like sex. And there's no reason why you can't cover all of that on the air for four hours a day. I'm trying to build an audience.

WE NOW INTERRUPT OUR REGULARLY SCHEDULED BROADCAST
FOR A WORD FROM...

JOE BELL, General manager, WQAM-Miami

I heard Sid on the FAN. Being in the business, I listen to a lot of different radio stations and I was a fan of the FAN, no pun intended. I listened to him there, and then when I took over WQAM in January 2006 he had just started in Miami at 790 The Ticket just a month before. When I heard him on 790, I wasn't yet the general manager of WQAM. When they made me the general manager, I went to our programming guys and asked how he got down here without us hiring him. I made it a point to get to know him, because I figured at some point in our paths would cross.

What is it they say? You keep your friends close and your enemies closer. I could see that what he did would work here. He did a nice job at 790. Neil Rogers did 10:00 AM to 2:00 PM here forever, and we parted company when Neil took an early retirement in June 2009. That coincided with Sid's situation, and it just was the perfect time to bring him over to QAM. Not only does Sid do sports, but he is able to talk about anything, do it intelligently, and do it well. He brings a dimension that some of the sports talk guys—I wouldn't say they don't have, but it's just not their thing. He'll talk politics, pop culture, and he's got an incredible sports knowledge. We've got Joe Rose in the morning and Jim Mandich in the afternoon, both former Dolphins players, so a lot of our talk skews to the Dolphins. And rightfully so, since we're the flagship. But I wanted to bring him in kind of as a counterpoint to those guys. He's edgier and he certainly has that New York vibe going on, which is big in South Florida. There are a lot of native New Yorkers living in South Florida. You know the joke about Florida, don't you? When you start at the northern end of Florida you're pretty much in the Deep South, and the farther south you go the farther north you get so that by the time you get to Boca you're back in New York. Down in Miami, people from New York seem to like that a lot, and they can relate to what Sid says. If there's a criticism from the Dolphins diehards, it's that Sid talks too much about the Giants and Jets and New York. I don't agree with that, obviously. I think what he does is fine, otherwise I wouldn't have hired him.

He won't be alone on his show because, you know, he's best friends with every celebrity in America, particularly those on the B- and C-list, so he will have his great friend *fill in the blank* on a regular basis. He does not have a cohost. He doesn't need one.

Nobody ever has *carte blanche*. We certainly give guidance, but he'll have a little bit more leeway than most on what to talk about. You can only talk about the same game for so many hours in a day. You need to have somebody to bring a little different perspective to the table, and that's what he'll do.

I just expect him to have a good sense of what people are talking about. It may be the Dolphins, it could be a lot of things, but we're always going to be a sports station. We need to be true to that, but he's got the ability to weave these other elements into his show. Best I know, Sid is the only person that's ever been a quasi-regular with Stern and Imus. I don't know anybody else that's friendly with both of them. It's very interesting.

Anybody who would tell you that he didn't have any trepidation with Sid would be lying to you, but he's an open book. That's what I like about him so much. He's right up front about what his problems have been and what he's done about them. That's one of the things I really like about him. But, yes, I'm more concerned for him personally. There's always going to be another talk show host you can hire. My real concern is I just want him to be healthy, and I think he is. I'm very comfortable bringing him over. I have to go by what I've observed and what I've heard. I've talked to a number of people that are pretty close to him, and I have no reason to believe those are still issues. Although we all know that when you have addictions I don't think you ever get over it, you deal with it. There's always a chance I'm sure of a relapse, but hopefully that won't be the case.

We had some pretty frank discussions, and that will be an area of focus. I told him "You're a great talent. You don't want to lose a job over something silly." We've been pretty clear what he can do and what he can't do, and I think he'll be fine. I turbocharged the dump button for Sid. We beefed that baby up. He'll be fine. He's a smart broadcaster.

The competitor, 790, was put on the air by a rich kid playing radio named Joel Feinberg. He lost millions, and Lincoln Financial took them back over two years ago. They're good operators; they run great radio stations. The competition when Joel had the station was very much on a personal level. He used to send me e-mails about how bad we sucked and things like that. That's all gone. Now they're good competitors. Their radio station is driven by *The Dan LeBatard Show*, and LeBatard's a real talent. I think he's very good and very formidable opposition. But I love the lineup we have. We have Joe Rose, the former Dolphin, in the morning; then Sid; then a guy named the Big O, Orlando Alzugaray; and then Jim Mandich, another former Dolphin, who has announced he's going to retire at the end of next year.

I was shocked when Sid became available. It just never crossed my mind that they would let him go. I was glad he became available, because it solved a need of mine. I was told that Sid had a Joe Bell clause in his contract with 790. I think they knew I liked him. I didn't make any secret about it. Like LeBatard, I think Sid is a real talent, and those two guys on that station concerned me. I told our guys that I always thought he did a great show. I'm just glad we're able to find a spot for him at QAM.

If you grow up in New York and you're a baseball player, I think your dream is always to play for the Yankees. I'm sure if the right opportunity came along he would love to go back to the FAN. I think it's either Miami or New York, and right now it's Miami.

The Parent Trap

It's bullshit, clichéd nonsense when everybody says they're close to their parents. Not everybody's so close to their parents. But I am very, very close to mine, Naomi and Harvey.

My father was a big-time sports fan growing up. A Giants and Dodgers fan living in Coney Island, he always wanted a son. My parents had two daughters, Alana and Raysheri, before I came along 12 years later. After me came my baby sister Alizabeth, but I was the only son, the prince.

I suffered a very bad asthma attack when I was five weeks old, and I was a very sickly kid growing up. I always demanded a lot of attention. My asthma was serious. I wasn't one of those kids who you could throw an inhaler at or who could take a couple of pills and be good to go. I had it so bad that often times I had to be rushed straight to the emergency room to have adrenaline pumped into my body. I was like that from the age of five weeks old until I was about 17 or 18. My mom sat up with me at night, with the humidifier and the medicine. My parents were deathly afraid that I was going to die, literally.

That didn't stop my father from turning me into a big sports fan as a young kid. I played Little League everything: baseball, basketball, football. My first Little League Baseball team was North Highway Little League at Kings Highway in Brooklyn, and then I went on to play Kings Bay baseball and Kings Bay football. I was asthmatic, I was skinny, and I was sick all the time, but I was the starting defensive end for the Kings Bay Blue Jays football team. We went undefeated and unscored-upon all year long. How many skinny, Jewish, asthmatic defensive ends are out there? After that, I went to play for the Redskins of Kings Bay. There I became a really good football player. I actually went to the All-Star team that year, and my father was the coach along with Harold Waxman.

My father always coached the teams. He coached me in baseball, basketball, and football. Not every kid can say that. I know my mom wasn't thrilled about me playing tackle football when I was an asthmatic as a young kid, but my dad made sure I did it—and I loved it. He was a very active parent, very involved in my life. Today I see all these parents out here in suburbia, and they all want to take credit: "My kid does this; my kid does that." The parents drop them off, and once in a while they show up for a game. My dad was there from the beginning to the end. It was a loving approach, and it was always about having fun on his teams. *Winners never quit and quitters never win* was always cemented into my mind as a young kid, but so was the emphasis on having fun. My dad knew I wasn't going to be a professional ballplayer. He never acted like those asshole parents who start fights with other parents and rough up their kids, either.

The one time I got upset with my dad, I was playing football for the Redskins, and he wanted me to take a pitchout. I was okay at taking handoffs, but pitchouts scared the shit out of me because once, in practice, I got a pitchout and by the time I caught the ball, the defensive linemen nailed me good. I was 10 or 11, and our opponent had this one big kid. He was like the best defensive player in the whole Little League. My father called for a pitchout in the huddle. I started to cry and said, "I'm telling mommy and I'm going home. I'm not doing it." My father said, "C'mon, Sidney, stop. We practiced this. You can do it." Sure enough, I took the pitchout and I had a long run. That was about the only time my father got on me.

My mom grew up on Kings Highway and my Dad grew up in Coney Island. I'm very close to my mom and my three sisters. It's a very tight-knit family, my three brothers-in-law Albert, Harry, and Michael. When I got accepted to the University of Miami, pre-med, my family was elated. Then, three months later I came home 40 pounds less and without one credit to my name. I never went to class, was literally hooked on drugs. They sent away their nice Jewish son to the University of Miami expecting him to soar, and I was home in the most embarrassing of situations three months later.

My mom was really the reason I ultimately graduated college. I enrolled in Brooklyn College for a little while and the results were the same. I was still going out at night and drinking and doing coke and not taking school seriously. Brooklyn College was a complete and utter disaster. I was a kid who was considered brilliant in high school. I was in the top percentile of all these tests I took, I was the president of my high school, and I had almost a 90 average. And then I went away to college and went to two colleges with nothing to show for it. It was my mom who saved that.

I was really hooked on my girlfriend at the time and all I wanted to do was spend time with her. I even stopped doing coke and drinking during that time because she threatened to break up with me. I had left two colleges and was working for her father in a women's clothing store on Reade Street in the city. My mother told me, "You have to go back to school. You're a smart kid, you have all these aspirations, and you're wasting your time." We were fortunate, because at that time Kingsborough Community College had just started up a thing called the New Start program, in which it took kids who had gone to other schools and failed and literally let them start over. I went in with a clean slate. My mother got me in, I eventually got my two-year degree, and I went on to graduate from Baruch. It took me four schools and seven years to graduate, but I did it.

There were those moments when my parents would sit up and wait for me till 5:00, 6:00, 7:00, 8:00, 9:00 in the morning. The sun would be coming out, everybody would be on their way to work, and I was still out. I'd walk in the door at 8:30 in the morning completely fucked up, and my parents would be sitting there going, "What the fuck are you doing?"

I've been to rehab twice. The first time in Wernersville, Pennsylvania, at Chit Chat Farms. They had a whole day when you just sat in a room with your parents and basically just yelled and screamed and cried with each other, to figure out what the hell was going on. We had lots of those moments, but they never gave up on me. They never threw me out.

There were times in my life when they played a lesser role— especially when I was dating Ava and not going to school and wasn't home all that much. I had kind of cut them out then, but they never cut me out—ever. Those were some rough years, between 1984 and 1992 when I got married, and the rough years continued after I got married. I put Danielle through a lot of garbage and my parents too. After I got married, Danielle took the brunt of it, but my parents sat in on a lot of rough days and a lot of rough discussions.

I like my parents. As a son, you're always obligated to love your parents. Even kids who are neglected and abused eventually say, "I still love my parents." I don't know what it is. But I also like my parents. Look, they got their *shtiklech*, they got their *meshugass* like everybody else, but I like them. They're good people. There are a lot of things we enjoy and have in common. We can sit down even at this stage of the game and discuss a variety of topics and have fun.

My father turned 75 in 2009. My parents are going on nearly 60 years of marriage, and it's amazing. Do they have the perfect marriage? Or course not. Who the fuck does? But at the end of the day, they have four kids and 12 grandchildren. My niece, Tamara, is pregnant with their first great-grandchild.

The Worst Words in the English Language: "No More Daddy"

I was driving my family from Florida up to New York on July 10, 2009. My parents have their summer house up in White Plains, and we've been going there for more than 30 years. We love it there. I like to drive up from Florida. This way, Danielle has the car up there in case she and the kids want to do something. Along the way we stopped in Charlotte, North Carolina, to visit Danielle's stepfather. She still has a good relationship with him. We figured we'd stop in Carolina on Friday, spend the weekend, and then Monday morning head up to New York.

When we arrived in North Carolina that night, I sent a text to my father, telling him that we got there safely and that we were looking forward to seeing him soon. When I send my father a text, he gets back to me in five minutes—every time. So a half an hour goes by, an hour goes by, and nothing. So I called the house upstate, and my niece Maxxe picked up the phone.

I said, "Hi Maxxe, put Poppy on the phone," because all his grandchildren and nieces and nephews call him Poppy. She said, "He can't come to the phone. He's not breathing. He's unresponsive."

"What are you talking about?" I said. "I just spoke to Daddy yesterday. What do you mean he's unresponsive?"

She said, "The ambulance is here, but he's not breathing."

"Maxxe, put somebody else on the fucking phone."

So she put my cousin Kandi on. "Oh my God, Sidney. He's not answering us. He's not awake."

"Put my brother-in-law on the phone, Kandi." So she put my brother-in-law Albert on the phone, and he basically tells me that my father is a sick man.

"What do you mean he's a sick man? He was healthy for 75 years up until last night. How all of a sudden does he become a very sick man?"

At the time, nobody knew what the hell was going on. All they knew was that his fever had spiked to 106, he was unconscious, and they were slapping an IV on him and rushing him to Harris Hospital in Monticello. They were able to figure out that he had some type of bad infection. They also knew they couldn't treat him at Harris Hospital and needed to get him out of there, because at that point his heart had become an issue. So they airlifted him from Monticello to Westchester Medical Center, which isn't more than a 40-minute trip. We later found out that he died in that helicopter. He flatlined not once but twice, and they had to paddle him back to life in the helicopter.

When he got to Westchester he was in a coma. I called all night, texted all night, wanted to know if I should fly there. We decided to drive to New York early the next morning. Everyone kept telling us that nothing was new, he was still unconscious, and they were still doing tests. I came to find out later that they were told by the cardiologist that because of the infection my dad had suffered a massive heart attack and that he was basically dead. His kidneys weren't working, his liver wasn't working, and he was pretty much finished. Danielle drove. We spent the next 10 hours in the car, and I just looked out the window and cried for 10 straight hours. I was thinking, *I'm not going to the cemetery, and I'm not doing the eulogy. I'm his best friend, and he's my best friend, but I'm not going*, because I knew I wouldn't be able to handle it.

I remember going to the second floor of the hospital, the medical intensive care unit, and my mother running toward me saying, "Oh my God, Sidney, no more Daddy, no more Daddy. Daddy's gone." I didn't want to go into the room. My cousin Stephen was there, and he turned to me and said, "Go in there and talk to him. They think he can hear you." I walked into the room and I just fell to my knees. He had 20 tubes in him! He just had that look of death. I composed myself and I talked to him. That was Saturday. That Saturday, Sunday, Monday, and Tuesday I never went home and I never slept. I stayed in the hospital in the waiting room, sitting on a wooden chair for four straight days with no sleep. I was afraid to leave because I thought he was going to die.

I sat with him that Sunday night for about three hours. Visiting hours were over at like 9:00, but the nurse let me sit with him until like 11:00 at night. I said to my mom, "I would say something, and Daddy would move his arm, move his leg." They kept telling me that's involuntary, that it could just be the medicine. I wasn't convinced. I would say something about my son, his grandson, only eight months old, and he would move his arm. I felt like it was something more than an involuntary jerk. I started to develop a little bit of optimism. The nurse kept telling me, hope for the best but expect the worst.

I kept seeing signs here and there of what I thought was him coming out of it. The nurse told us early Tuesday morning that while she was bathing him on Monday night his eyes opened. Just for a second, but then they shut, and he was back in a coma. I kept looking at these things as reasons to be optimistic. On Tuesday morning the nurse grabbed my mother and said, "Come with me, alone." My sisters and I waited outside. The nurse and my mother were hugging and crying, and no one knew if they were hugging and crying because my dad has passed away or what. My sisters were saying, "What do you see. What do you see?" and I said to them, "I don't know. I see the nurse crying. Mommy went inside into the room with Daddy. Maybe there's something good here." Literally five minutes later the nurse walked out and said, "Go say hello to your father."

We were still under the impression at that point that he had suffered a massive heart attack. He had one eye open and one eye closed. He couldn't talk, he had a feeding tube in his mouth, but he was smiling, and he was gesturing with his hands. But we were still very nervous. He had woken up, which was an amazing thing, but we weren't confident it was going to be okay. The doctors were telling us he was not close to being out of the woods. His kidney levels were bad, his liver levels were terrible, and his heart was still a mess. As it turned out, he never had a heart attack at all, even though the cardiologist told us so. He had three infections, one deadly enough to kill him. He had two strands of E-coli and one tick bite, believe it or not, that he carried around for about a year. The infections masked the tests to make it look like he had a heart attack. Instead, the infections shut down all of his major organs.

A month and a half later he was doing well. He went back to work, driving. It took time for him to regain his strength, and he still goes to the cardiologist and the doctor all the time. We found out after all this time that he was diabetic, something we didn't know for 75 years. Now he watches his diet and takes his blood two or three times a day. So he didn't come out of the episode unscathed, but in the end there was no real damage to any of his major organs. He's still, thank God, a relatively healthy guy.

It's not that I appreciate my dad any more or my mom any more than I did before because of what happened. I've always loved them. But I am now more aware of the people I love. They tend to get thrown aside in this fucking chaotic life of ours, especially mine. I can get so worried about the new job and Facebook and Twitter and sidrosenberg.com and all that fucking nonsense, but I find myself talking to my dad every day. I wasn't the one who was sick, but that feeling of loss for those couple of days and couple of weeks was so fucking profound that I definitely look at things differently. I'm not as caught up in the bullshit and the nonsense as I once was.

I never believed in God. I went to Yeshiva as a kid and I had a bar mitzvah and I did and said all the right things but I mother-fucked God up and down in rehab. I remember sitting there the last time, in 2005, saying, "What kind of fucking God lets somebody fly an airplane into a building and kill 3,000 people?" The priest said to me, "Those men took God's will into their own hands. He's a loving God." It just seemed too convenient. He's a loving God. When something good happens, you thank God, but when something bad happens, you say, "Oh, that's someone taking God's will in their own hands." What kind of bullshit is that? There I was in fucking rehab, I had a young daughter (this was before my son was born), I'm a good person and a nice guy, and I got all these fucking issues. My life was a mess.

There's no fucking God. When we were driving from North Carolina back to New York to see my dad, there was a big billboard of Jesus Christ and it said, "If you are in despair...find Jesus now." I was hysterical crying, and I looked over at Danielle and said, "If this is going to save Daddy's life, that's fine. Help me Jesus, help me somebody. God just help me." I'm not a religious person, barely even a spiritual person. But I found myself in the waiting room at 4:00 AM asking God for help, because I was desperate. When he woke up I told my cousin Kandi, "Now I'm a believer."

Look, I'm not going to *shul* every single day. It's not as if all of a sudden I'm joining the Lubavitch. But I do believe now that it wasn't just the antibiotics that killed my dad's infection. I do believe there was somebody out there looking out for him. I really do believe that there was some type of divine intervention. I'm not changing my lifestyle. This is not, *Oh my God, I found God, now I'm going to run to Israel and live on a kibbutz for three years.* That ain't gonna happen. But I honestly do believe there was somebody out there looking out for him.

Everyone's a Critic, Especially the Assholes

I think the business sucks. I'm an angry guy, in a sense. I'm told by people all the time that I'm as talented as anybody in the business, *blah blah blah*. I've been out of work a couple times, obviously. Even though certain hosts and certain stations wanted to hire me, there's always some guy wearing a fucking suit and tie who doesn't know dick about radio that inevitably makes the decision to not hire me. It frustrates and angers me that people can't take radio for what it is.

I readily admit that I have said stuff that's been offensive and hurtful and irresponsible. I would certainly take back what I said about Kylie Minogue or the Williams sisters. But at the same time, why do people get so fucking angry? People hold this shit against you forever, whether it's radio executives who are in charge of hiring or firing, or fans, or the media. They just keep bringing this shit up over and over, and eventually the label sticks. I'm on the air for five hours a day. At one point at the FAN, I was on the air for nearly nine hours a day. The No. 1 station in radio, and I owned about nine hours a day of real estate between the *Imus* show and my midday show. Eight and a half, to be exact. When you're on the air for eight and a half hours a day, every now and then you're going to say something stupid. That's just the way it is.

The conservative talk radio host Michael Savage has said some horrible things along the way. Imus has been in trouble. Howard Stern, I love the guy, but the shit that he says is unreal. Now he's on satellite, so he's not governed by the FCC, but the shit he did over the years was hard to believe. When guys are making lots and lots of money they kind of look the other way. Imus got fired inevitably, I know that, but he went to ABC and the Fox Business Network and he's doing great again. The big guys, they find a way to stay up. Bill O'Reilly is full of shit. He's done some stuff over the years that has been absolutely reprehensible, and yet he sits there on Fox News every single night acting like he's the country's moral compass. The hypocrisy that's out there is just hard to believe.

They label you. *Sid said that thing about Venus Williams. He must be a racist.* I'm the furthest thing from a racist. Tiki Barber came up to me and said that was the funniest thing he ever heard, what I said about Venus Williams. Tiki, the former Giants running back—a black guy, by the way. I can't tell you how many people weren't mad at me about that, who thought it was funny. People don't look at the body of work. They hear one thing, and that's what you become.

There were times at the FAN, obviously, where there were serious issues—times when I was suspended, times when I was fired. But it got to the point where, after a while, my phone would ring, it would be Chernoff, and I'd be like, "Oh God, now what?" A lot of times it would be something totally innocuous, totally silly. The problem is that once I got that reputation, once somebody labeled me—like that piece of shit Phil Mushnick of the *New York Post* or that moron Bob Raissman of the *Daily News* and all these guys writing about how bad I am—every little thing I said was scrutinized. I've been out of New York almost five years, and I'm still reading a story from Phil Mushnick about Craig Carton and how the radio industry has really gone to hell with all the no-talents on the air. He wrote, "Sid Rosenberg's only discernable talent was to be a lowlife for Imus." After the Mushnicks, the

Raissmans, the fans and the executives labeled me, that was it. I could say something that was really no big deal and it'd be, "Come into my office." After a while I got anxiety attacks. I would see Chernoff's name on my phone and I'd freak out.

I've been told to dial it back, and when I've done that, the results haven't been good. Working with Don Imus and other places when I would dial it back—and it would be obvious I was holding back—some of the same people who complained that I was too crazy would complain that now I'd gotten too generic, too vanilla. When I got out of rehab in 2005 and I came back to the *Imus* show and the show with Joe Benigno, I was different. I was not going to say anything too crazy, and Imus complained. "Oh my God, where's the old Sid? You know, the Sid that used to smoke crack? That guy was crazy, that guy was funny. This new Sid, this new AA/NA Sid is not the same," he'd say. I knew he didn't mean that in his heart of hearts. I knew he wanted the best for me personally, but he really wanted that guy on the show that was going to be unpredictable.

There were times when I scaled it back and the hosts I was working with or the fans actually complained, because they were used to a certain guy. They were used to a guy going on the air and saying, "Jeromy Burnitz is a piece of shit" or calling people douchebags and scumbags. When I wasn't doing that type of stuff, it wasn't ringing true. So I always found myself in a catch-22: if I scaled it back too much, then there was nothing to differentiate me from everybody else on the air, which for the most part is garbage.

Sports talk, for the most part, is crap. It's fucking nonsense. There are a lot of guys on the air who are just not that talented, end of story. Not so at the FAN. I think Francesa, Benigno, Sommers, those guys all have talent. But I've worked in different cities across America, and the talent is marginal at best. I think what happens is guys, when they know a lot about sports, they think that makes them a good talk show host, but it doesn't. All it means is that you know a lot about sports. I worked in Miami with Dan LeBatard, and I think he does a good job because his show, although it's a sports show, delves into everything that I delve into: politics, pop culture, entertainment. He doesn't take himself too seriously. And although he's completely capable of having a great sports conversation, he doesn't get caught in the minutiae every single day.

There's no credibility with a guy like Mushnick. He hates everybody. In the last 10 years, the four guys he has written the most about are Imus, Francesa, Craig Carton, and me. Imus and Francesa built FAN to be the most successful radio station in the history of the medium. Say what you want about Craig Carton, but the last time I checked, he and Boomer Esiason were No. 1 in men ages 25–54 in New York. Mushnick doesn't like anybody who has success. But he'll write about a weekend guy who nobody gives a flying fuck about, and he'll give them all the credit in the world in his column and call him the next Marv Albert. To me, that's a guy who's just envious. I don't know if he thinks he should be on the radio or what. It's no coincidence that all the guys who have a lot of success are the same guys he writes about. And he gets downright personal. I've seen my name in those columns even recently. When he gets a hard-on for somebody, he doesn't let it go. I'm not in New York anymore, Mushnick. Leave me the fuck alone.

Bob Raissman came up with the nickname "Mad Dog" for Chris Russo, and he called me "Sidiot" for years and years. I guess it was cute the first hundred times, but after a while, what the fuck? My problem is, it gets personal after a while. I remember reading the Sunday paper for those five or six years in New York, and it would be ridiculous. I've been told any publicity is good publicity, but that's not true in my case. It was true to a certain extent, because after the Venus Williams thing everybody kind of stood up for me and Imus rehired me. But my bad publicity continues to plague me, there's no question about it. It has cost me opportunities at good jobs. Has my bad publicity put my name out there? Yes. Do sports fans know who I am? Yes. I'm still on *Imus* in 2010, and I made that Venus and Serena comment on Imus in 2001. So yes, there are certain places where that "bad publicity" has kept me going, but there are also places where that bad publicity has literally gotten me blackballed.

You can criticize me; that's one thing. If you want to go out there and say, "Sid, you shouldn't have said that. That was lowbrow, offensive, and horrible," I have no problem with that. But when you hold a grudge and it becomes personal, that's when I get upset. During the years that I was up in New York I don't think there was anybody—including Francesa and Imus—in the papers more than me between Mushnick and Raissman. I was in those columns every week. Even Steve Zipay in *Newsday* beat the shit out of me. It was a fucking free-for-all. Imus, whether you like him or not, is one of the legends of the business. He's still making $13 million, so he must be doing something right. I've been on the show for eight years. I sat with Howard Stern in his studio on Sirius, and he told me, "You're good. You obviously have the gift for gab." I was for five years the host of the midday show and the Giants on WFAN, and by their own admission I could have been there for 20 years. I could have been Francesa's sidekick right now.

It would be one thing if they beat me up for two weeks and then they wrote about a good interview I'd had. I never read that. Not once. I've heard Ed Coleman on the FAN for 20 years. Nobody had the back-and-forth with Ed like I did. Coleman has told me that. Did I ever read that in Raissman and Mushnick? Never. Jerome from Manhattan has been calling the station for 100 years. The best Jerome call ever was with me. Did that make Bob Raissman's column? No. But every time something went wrong, those two were the first to kick me in the teeth. That's where I get angry. You can't tell me I didn't do something right all those years. Raissman fucking knows I'm good. Mushnick fucking knows I'm good. But you know what? After you start writing bad about somebody over and over again for years and years and years, you're almost stuck in that quagmire.

Barry Jackson is down in Miami for the *Miami Herald*, and he covers me like Mushnick and Raissman did. But he is a fair guy. I didn't like the fact that, when I first got down to Miami, every time they wrote about me they included all that *Imus* shit. I understand that it's part of my resume and part of who I am. At least Barry has said some nice things about me. Tom Jicha from the *Fort Lauderdale Sun Sentinel* calls me "colorful but controversial," and he writes nice things. In Miami, Jackson and Jicha have both been rough on me, absolutely, but they've found things in my shows that they've liked and they've written about. At least they have some type of credibility.

WE NOW INTERRUPT OUR REGULARLY SCHEDULED BROADCAST FOR A WORD FROM...

PHIL MUSHNICK, Radio and TV critic, *New York Post*

What good could I possibly have written about him? When you say "Sid Rosenberg," I think, *professional creep*. He was never funny, never clever, never creative. His talent was lodged in his nerve. If you can make a living saying things that most people wouldn't have the nerve to say because they're right-headed and civil-minded, then Sid Rosenberg's the guy. He deals in shock, and that's tired. It's the same radio formula, that "morning zoo" formula over and over. Some guys are good at it. Some guys can tell a dirty joke and make you laugh. Other guys can just be dirty and think that passes as humor and creativity.

He says, "Look how far I made it." The formula is to be shocking. You don't have to be good. Just say what nobody else has the nerve to say. Something low. Go as low as you possibly can, and you'll get a job, then they'll suspend you. How can he possibly reconcile or rationalize or be proud of the fact that he would make fun of people with all sorts of afflictions? It was always crotch humor. The Australian singer, Kylie Minogue, had a mastectomy, and he's making a vulgar joke about titties? That's not funny. What kind of skill is that? That he was suspended was not a shame on Sid; it was a shame on the station and the management because they suspended him for the same reason they hired him: to go low. He went too low? Well, that's their fault. I don't blame Sid for that. In his defense, these are the terms of his engagement. Go low. He's not even any good at it.

He was a host of a sport talk show where he said, "Take the points, 3½, I'd go with this." Here's a guy with a profound gambling problem who owed everybody in town money, and he's getting on the air giving his picks. I mean, think about that. What is his skill? Shock. If you call that a skill, then he's a very skilled guy.

I lump him in with Craig Carton. The bottom line is that of all the guys FAN could have hired to replace Imus, they hire Carton. Imus at least made you laugh once in a while. Carton just aims for the crotch and he stays there. The ratings are high, but I think it's a matter of competition. Fans turn to where sports is spoken. There's very little competition, and I think FAN to its credit has always been a habit turn-on. When I write about guys like Rosenberg, I get 900 e-mails from people who despise the guy, but they still listen, and they're hoping for better around him. They're not listening for him, they're listening around him, they're listening in spite of him. Of all the e-mails and phone messages and letters I've ever received supportive of Carton and Rosenberg, that type, it's always self-fulfilling. It's always "Suck my dick" or "Eat shit and die" or "Sid rules, you suck." It becomes exactly my point. This is who he appeals to.

I was a Howard Stern fan when he was funny, as opposed to crude. Eventually the crudity began to outweigh the humor. I always thought he was creative. He would make me laugh out loud. I'd sit at a red light and see everybody laughing because they're listening to Stern. But once it became "We're lesbians, let's lick each other," that's not funny. Albert Brooks did a bit where he was doing a stand-up routine in Texas and he was bombing, and then he decided to yell out "Fuck," and the place went, "Whooooooo, that guy is funnnnny!" That's Sid Rosenberg. If you think he's funny, you think yelling out "fuck" is funny.

I am a TV/radio critic with an emphasis on sports. I can either ignore Sid, which I did most of the time, or write about him. What could I possibly write good about him? That he has succeeded because he's mastered the art of the modern radio marketing formula of being a professional creep? I've written that.

WE NOW INTERRUPT OUR REGULARLY SCHEDULED BROADCAST
FOR A WORD FROM...

MARK LEPSELTER, President, Maxx Sports
& Entertainment and Sid Rosenberg's agent

As far as what I would say to his critics, on the *Imus* show, did Sid take it too far at times? Yes, he did. Did he force the issue too much to draw attention to himself because he so badly wanted to perform for Imus, and because he wanted to be a star? Yes, he did. Those were toxic things. Sid always told me, Don pushed him at times. If he wasn't funny or over-the-top on certain days that Imus would break his balls and say, "That's it, I'm bringing Carlin in," or "You're not getting the job done." Sid played a role on *Imus* that he probably played too well. He was the henchman on the show. Then he could flip the switch at 10:00 and go on with Jody Mac or Joe Benigno and be a different guy, a legitimate, entertaining sports guy.

Lawrence Taylor has a great line: "It's very easy for the guys with the notepads to throw the darts." The Raissmans, the Mushnicks generally don't have anything positive to say, whereas others, like Neil Best of *Newsday*, are objective. Sid gave writers constant fodder. He was such a lightning rod. He certainly created many of his own headaches. At one time, Sid's attitude was, "Screw it, any ink is good ink." I think he's matured and understands that is not necessarily the case anymore.

When I met Sid he was already at FAN. Joe Benigno put Sid in touch with me. My first impressions of him?: He was certainly a unique and interesting character. It was very clear to me that he absolutely thought there was no one better on the radio than him and that he was going to be a big star in that world. He was a very hyper, jumpy dude. I was like, *What the fuck is wrong with this guy?* I didn't know the extent of his personal issues but I was aware of them. I thought I could help him in that regard as well.

As his star rose, every time he would take one step forward, he would always take two steps back. He was the master fuck-up artist but it was part of what made Sid Sid. He would have his moments on the air, he'd say something, and I'd get a call. He was like your younger child who was constantly getting in trouble at school. I liken it to L.T. Lawrence would go off track during the week, but he knew he could make it right on Sunday. Sid was like that. He'd mess up but he knew he could make it okay the next morning on the air. There's no one I've done more for as a client, as far as time and effort and being nimble in my representation. And it has been extremely gratifying for me because I know how much these opportunities have meant for Sid and his family.

Have people said to me over the years that I should cut Sid loose, that he's not worth the trouble? Yes. But for me, there's a personal relationship we've had for close to 10 years. I have a responsibility to protect him as his friend and represent him as his agent. Has it been a roller coaster ride? A hundred percent. Are there things Sid's done that I haven't agreed with? Absolutely. Have I earned every dime I've made? *Abso-fucking-lutely.* Professionally, I have no problem acknowledging my hope is that everything will come together for him. Why should I let someone else revel in that when I put in all the blood, sweat, and tears?

His image of himself is *nobody loves Sid more than Sid.* It's kind of a neurotic insecurity combined with an enormous ego. He's always looking over his shoulder at the next thing. He's got such grandiose ideas, he's very creative, he's a very smart guy, very well-read, and he can speak about a lot of different things—that's what makes him such an entertaining radio host. I absolutely believe that had he not shot himself in the foot all those times, he would be an enormous star, on the top level just underneath the real legends of radio, the Imuses and the Sterns.

I know I get criticized for the Atlantic City deal. We drove down in my car—God forbid Sid drove down in his car, because then he would have to pay for the gas. He is the cheapest SOB on the face of the earth. I remember sitting on the boardwalk with him, hanging out. It was in September, it was a beautiful day, and he was fine. We went back to the hotel, cleaned up, and went to the Foundation Room in the Showboat Hotel, where *FHM* was hosting this party. The party had a really good vibe. I was totally on Sid, the *FHM* guys were all buddies of mine, and they were watching him as well. He may have had *a* drink but he was completely sober. After we left the party, I left him in the lobby of the hotel and told him, "Dude, we're out of here at such-and-such time in the morning." He had to get back to do the Giants pregame show on FAN. The rest is history. The next morning I started calling his cell phone and he wasn't answering. I went to his room, I walked in, took a look at him, and I just knew.

I told Sid, "Get dressed, we need to get out of here," but he was unresponsive. He was as strung-out as one could be. I all but grabbed him, but he would not go. I waited and waited. Finally I got him to come down to the lobby. I said, "You better get in a cab. I'm heading up north." I absolutely exhausted everything I could to get him to leave with me, but he would not do it. I prayed he would get in a cab and get to the Meadowlands. I was driving on the parkway, avoiding calls from Mark Chernoff. At whatever time he was due at the stadium, he was not there. I finally answered the call and told Chernoff that he wasn't going to be there. Chernoff met me downstairs by the suites at the stadium and told me, "It's over. He's fired."

I told Sid, I am not his brother. I am not his father. Yes, I'm his friend and his agent. It is very easy to throw darts in that situation, but I don't give a damn who you are. If you want to party, you're going to find a place to party. It doesn't matter if it's Atlantic City or Iowa City. It's very easy to say that Sid shouldn't have been in Atlantic City. Sid wanted to do Atlantic City. He wasn't going to pass up on the paycheck.

A few days later Sid came by my house to pick up his car. My wife, Amy, was home and they talked about the situation. She told Sid a story about a close family member who had the same issues with substance abuse and who had subsequently passed away. Sid was preparing to leave town and take his family to Florida. She told him he had to get his life together for his wife and daughter. Sid was very emotional and before he left he handed her a $25 chip from Resorts that he had with him from the weekend in Atlantic City. He said, "I'll do my best." To the best of everyone's knowledge, since that day Sid has been clean.

Conclusion, or, Here's Where I Do What I Do Best: Get the Last Word

I think I'm in a good place.

Look, I'm an addict and I have obsessive compulsions. None of that ever goes away. Do I wake up every single day and feel like everything is grand? No. My life is not perfect yet. Not because everything around me isn't perfect. It is. My wife, my children, my family, my job now...all that is great. But I still battle with myself because I have so many different compulsions that kind of sneak into my life every single day. I certainly have more serenity (if you want to use that word) and more peace than I've had in a long, long time, and I feel like I'm on the right path. So, I would say things right now are really good. Especially when you read this book and see all the tumult and all the horror that I put myself through all those years, I think I'm in a much better place now.

What did I learn about myself? That I was pretty fucked up. The one thing about me is, I've always known I had issues. I'd go to a 12-step, meeting and somebody would say, "I didn't know I was a drunk. I didn't know I was an alcoholic. I didn't know I was an addict." I've always known. For me, the compulsion, at times, was just too much; I couldn't stop it.

I'm happy. There are some people in the book (and I've repaired some of those relationships) from some of the early days of my career. There are some people who will look at me in a different light, and that's good. People inside the business have always felt, *Sid's not perfect, Sid's not an angel, Sid is always going to be a little crazy, but that's part of the appeal.* But I think a lot of people in the book are now in a comfortable place with me, too, which is a good thing.

I would hope they like me. Here are the facts: The worst things I've done in my life have been gambling, losing money, borrowing money from people and being a little slow in getting it back. Those are my worst crimes. I've never killed anybody, raped anybody, stolen from anybody. I'm a good person. I've been told this time and again during my career, even by people who have been angry with me. Mike Francesa said it: It's almost impossible to stay angry with Sid. Everybody says that. Almost everybody in this book has been pissed off at me at some point, and yet I'm friends with just about everybody in the book. The people who know me know I'm a good person, a caring person. I've got some issues, and I haven't always made the right decisions; I've fucked up a couple of times along the way, and I'm not perfect. But then I never claimed I was.

That's why I wrote this book. I'm not afraid to tell people that I've got some issues. But I think you know I'm a good person. You can tell by my relationship with my parents, my relationship with my wife and children, my relationship with some of the biggest names in the industry. I think people will put down this book and think, *He's kind of a wild guy, he's kind of a crazy guy, but how can you not like him?*

There was a documentary made about the Miami Hurricanes football team. The current athletic administration at Miami was not involved in the movie. They wouldn't allow the head coach, Randy Shannon, to appear in the movie, and they didn't want the athletic director involved because there was some stuff in the movie the university would like to forget. What they don't realize is that's all part of the legend. The fact is, they were winning championships. There was a lot of crazy shit that went on during the

'80s and '90s but they were successful—they won five championships! There is a movie about them because they were great, and you can't just take the good stuff and throw away the other stuff. It's all part of the legend.

I'm not describing myself as a legend, but it's kind of the same thing. You can't take my New York success and Miami success, the Imus and the Stern and all of my professional success without the rest of the stuff that came with it. The school, the Hurricanes, did a bad job with that by trying to act like certain things never happened. With me, whether it's my daughter reading the book or my father or my next employer, I won't deny it; all of it happened. I won't hide it. To me, I just consider it part of the legend.

I can even tell you what the sequel is going to be. Despite blown opportunities and missed opportunities, I really, really believe the next book, the sequel, will be that all of my attainable goals that looked like they went up in smoke a couple of years ago will in fact come to fruition. Whether it's radio, TV, or my personal life, everything that seemed so attainable and right at my fingertips a couple of years ago is going to come back. Every dream I wanted to realize, I will. I'm going to be back—and bigger than ever. I'm guaranteeing that.

Editor's note:

Perhaps you can go home again.

On February 6, 2010, the day before Super Bowl XLIV, Sid Rosenberg hosted a show on FAN when he worked the 1:00–4:00 PM slot. It was the first time Rosenberg appeared on his former station as host of his own show since September 11, 2005. The show garnered positive reviews and certainly left one to wonder, *Is the day coming when there will be a reconciliation of this sometimes turbulent, always intriguing relationship?*

Maybe once again the Sid will hit the FAN.

Acknowledgments

A very special thank you to my most loyal friend, Kevin Canessa, for all the great work you do on www.sidrosenberg.com and Shovio. Thank you, my friend.

Special thanks to my producer at the Ticket, Andy King, and my current producer at WQAM, Marc Eisenberg. Also to Eddie Erickson, Sal Licata, Matt Deutsch, Eddie Scozzare, Steve Somers, Sweeny Murti, Ed Coleman, and Marc Malusis (WFAN); Julie Kanfer, Charles McCord, Lou Rufino, Rob Bartlett (Imus); Chris Jones, Georgia Beasley, Josh Darrow and Lee Feldman, Victor Bermudez, Black Moses, Amanda Kapp, and D.D. DeFelice (WQAM); Tom Alexander, Allyson Turner, Dean Grossman, Mike "the Hine" Sweeney, Mark Mariani, and Ross Levinsohn (SportsLine); Peter Gold (VegasInsider.com); Leslie Gold, Butch Brennan, Rocco Burro (Shovio); Dan LeBatard, John "Stugotz" Weiner, Marc Hochman, Mike Marchant, and John "Boog" Sciambi (the Ticket); Joe Rose, Jim Mandich, Orlando Alzugary, and Kevin Rogers (WQAM); and Jason Garcia (Opensports.com).

I would also like to thank my very first agent, Bobby Barad, as well as Zach Krantz (WQAM), Marc Mondry (MSG), Melissa Chusid and Michael Klein (Maxximum Marketing), Ed Bunnell

(Fox Sports), Peter Schwartz (play-by-play partner with the New York Dragons), John Minko (WFAN), Warner Wolf (WABC), Joel Feld (CSTV), Jeremy Coleman and Steve Cohen (Sirius/XM), Dave "Davey Paychecks" Marchetti and Barry Carpe (opensports.com), Marc Lawrence (playbook.com) and Adam Meyer (adamwins.com).

About the Co-Author

PAUL SCHWARTZ is a sportswriter for the *New York Post* who, since 1994, has covered the New York Giants as well as the past 17 Super Bowls. He is an honors graduate of the University at Albany and lives on the North Shore of Long Island, New York, with his wife, Jutta, and their two children, Elena and Jared. Schwartz is also the author of *Tales From the New York Giants Sideline*.